The
UNITED STATES,
CUBA,
and CASTRO

The
UNITED STATES,
CUBA,
and CASTRO

An Essay on the
Dynamics of Revolution
and the
Dissolution of Empire

by
William Appleman Williams

NEW YORK, 1962

Published by Monthly Review Press
333 Sixth Avenue, New York 14, N. Y.

Manufactured in the United States of America
Library of Congress catalog card number 62-22081

From an American radical,
with esteem and affection,
to the memory of the
most challenging conservative
of them all:

JOHN QUINCY ADAMS

America goes not abroad in search of monsters
to destroy . . . . She well knows that by once
enlisting under other banners than her own,
were they even the banners of foreign independence, she would involve herself, beyond the
power of extrication, in all the wars of interest
and intrigue, of individual avarice, envy, and
ambition, which assume the colors and usurp
the standard of freedom. . . . She might become
the dictatress of the world; she would no longer
be the ruler of her own spirit.

Fourth of July Oration, 1821.

Books by
WILLIAM APPLEMAN WILLIAMS
American-Russian Relations, 1781-1947 (1952)
The Shaping of American Diplomacy, 1750-1955 (1956)
The Tragedy of American Diplomacy (1959)
The Contours of American History (1962)
The United States, Cuba, and Castro (1962)

Acknowledgement

As anyone who has made the effort knows, serious research in contemporary history involves an extensive and subtle knowledge of many official and private publications. Very few, if any, writers possess such familiarity with all these sources.

I wish to express my deep appreciation to Miss Ruth Davis of the Wisconsin State Historical Society for her help in meeting and solving this problem. Much of her assistance, probably the most important part, has come over a period of years through her gentle yet rigorous tutoring in how to find important pieces of evidence in unsuspected places in the relatively unexploited terrain of government publications. She is the best guide I have ever known. But she has also made countless independent suggestions of a wonderfully perceptive character which led on to important information. And her unconquerable good humor and perkiness have saved many a day from being lost to the discouragement and even boredom that are the occupational hazards of sustained research.

It is with affection and respect that I thank her publicly for her significant contributions to my work.

CONTENTS

Introduction

Americans cherish many ideological axioms about democracy, but perhaps the most treasured one is the proposition that democracies do not start wars. Conscience would in this instance seem to be father to casuistry and fantasy. Not only did the United States begin the War of 1812 and the War with Mexico (by a blockade of Mexican troops on the Rio Grande), but it initiated two wars involving Cuba within the relatively short space of 63 years.

It is impossible either to understand the present impasse in American-Cuban relations, or to evaluate the recent books on Castro's Cuba by Theodore Draper, by Karl E. Meyer and Tad Szulc, and by Nicolas Rivero,[1] unless one begins with the central truth that Cuba was ours to lose. This uncomfortable fact cannot be wished away. Not even the most elaborate and sophisticated exercise in disingenuousness can in the end circumnavigate the existence of an American empire which included Cuba.

Had American policy in action between 1895 and 1959 actually been successful according to its own standards, then there would have been no Castro and no CIA invasion. The current argument about whether or not the United States should intervene in Cuba and other Latin American countries is ridiculously irrelevant. It has been intervening ever since the 1780's and is still doing so today. The real issue concerns whether or not *any* kind of intervention is capable of effecting the traditional and existing American objectives.

More of that later. It is first necessary to get straight on

1. Theodore Draper, *Castro's Revolution: Myths and Realities* (New York, Praeger, 1962); Karl E. Meyer and Tad Szulc, *The Cuban Invasion: The Chronicle of a Disaster* (New York, Praeger, 1962); and Nicolas Rivero, *Castro's Cuba: An American Dilemma* (Washington, D.C., Luce, 1962).

1

the long term intervention. Directly and indirectly, with ships and troops and with economic weapons, the United States established and enforced limits on Cuba's economic, political, and social affairs from 1898 to 1959. Castro has not freed Cuba from that power—it is merely being exercised in a different way. The United States is today not directly involved in shooting Cubans. It is merely denying them a market for their sugar and other goods, and refusing them even the opportunity to buy most American products. It is also very probably aiding those who are trying to subvert Castro's revolutionary government from within the island.

No one would learn much of this from Mr. Draper, although he is in favor of supporting the underground in Cuba. For the most part he simply ignores American relations with Cuba prior to 1959. In his only explicit discussion of this question, he is vague and primarily negative. The only other exception is an implicit one involved in his description of the Cuban political economy on the eve of Castro's victory. Even in that instance, however, he treats Cuba as a self-contained entity. To this extensive degree, Draper is the very model of the analyst as a man who compartmentalizes and isolates events and ideas, and causes and consequences, which cannot in fact be understood unless their interrelatedness is described and explained in considerable detail.

Draper's approach is indefensible by any standard, but particularly on the part of one who describes his work as "a continuing struggle on my part to understand the Cuban reality," who says in connection with the invasion of 1961 that he is "far more interested in the policy that led to the disaster than to the so-called failure of intelligence," and who reveals in March, 1962, that he has reconsidered the subject "at greater length than I have ever done before." By denying the causal relevance of the past, Draper denies himself (and his many readers) a large number of important insights into the present.

Meyer and Szulc exhibit a greater sense of the vital im-

2

portance of the nature of American-Cuban relations prior to 1959. They, too, advance an argument for supporting an anti-Castro underground, but they are also clearly troubled by the broad relationship between American policy and the development of the Cuban Revolution. They do not, however, explore that connection with any rigor or in any detail, and do not integrate such considerations into their analysis. For that matter, their final interpretation of Castro and the Revolution often contradicts their own explicit and implicit suggestions about the effects of American policy.

Meyer and Szulc have a somewhat better excuse than Draper. To begin with, they are writing about the invasion *per se* and not about the Revolution. And newspaper men, even the best of them, labor under great pressures to forget even today as soon as the deadline is met. But the excuses and the explanations do not solve the problem. On all counts, therefore, it is necessary to establish more perspective on the present crisis before it can be examined in detail.

1

The Epoch of Empire

The United States had no active interest in acquiring title to Cuba when revolution erupted across the island in 1895. For one thing, America's own house was in considerable disarray. The Panic of 1893 and the ensuing depression created serious and extensive social unrest, and raised the specter of revolution in the minds of a good many influential Americans.

Foreign policy matters were by no means ignored during the first part of the depression. Indeed, they were steadily winning an increasing and active amount of attention from farmers and workers as well as from businessmen and politicians. But Americans were looking primarily to the markets of Asia, not Cuba or Latin America, as the solution to the depression, which they had come to explain as the result of overcapacity and overproduction. President Grover Cleveland warned in 1894 that the Sino-Japanese War, and the threatened dismemberment of China, "deserves our gravest consideration by reason of its disturbance of our growing commercial interests." It is not at all surprising, therefore, that Cleveland's objective in Cuba was to help Spain "pacify the island."

This determination to "pacify the island" remained the basic policy of the United States from 1895 to the outbreak of war with Spain in April, 1898. As he neared the decision to go to war to make peace, McKinley told the Spanish that the mess in Cuba "injuriously affects the normal functions of business, and tends to delay the condition of prosperity to which this country is entitled." Cuba was thus defined as a causal factor in American democracy and prosperity, and Spain was charged with the responsibility for handling that element in a manner specified by the United States. There has been no

5

change in that American logic of externalizing good and evil. Russia has merely been substituted for Spain.

Contrary to the standard accounts of the coming of war in 1898, there was no great and sustained public and popular demand for violence in behalf of freeing the Cubans until *after* the sinking of the *Maine*. There was, however, a growing consensus among key business, labor, and political leaders on the necessity of "pacifying the island" in order to concentrate on the more important aspects of overseas economic expansion and domestic recovery.

Cuba did have some direct significance in the thinking of those men. The island commanded the European entrance to any projected canal, which was seen primarily as a means to capture the Asian trade. While American leaders preferred to have Spain retain a formal and effective measure of control over Cuba, they were not willing to allow a revolution to produce a shift in ownership to a strong European power. They were not, however, particularly worried that such was about to occur. In addition, businessmen were increasingly disturbed by the destruction of American property holdings, and the commerce attendant thereto, and steadily more interested in the possibility of expanding their operations under American aegis. And at least the leadership of the cigarmakers' unions wanted to free Cuba in order to expand their jurisdiction and thereby control the competition.

Two other aspects of the Cuban situation became ever more important, both relatively and absolutely, after the late summer of 1897. One was the growing fear that the Cuban revolutionaries would win a clear victory and thereby establish a government of what American leaders called "the troublesome, adventurous, and non-responsible class." That was undesirable and to be avoided. The second consideration involved the clear and increasing interest in acquiring the Philippines as a base for winning a predominant share in the markets of China.

Theodore Roosevelt and his imperialist cronies were by no

means the only Americans who wanted the Philippines. After all, the McKinley Administration did not revoke Theodore's famous orders to Commodore George Dewey in November, 1897, to stand ready to take the Philippines, which TR had dispatched one afternoon when he usurped the powers of his superiors. McKinley himself had discussed the crucial importance of the islands with many key leaders as early as September, 1897; and the President dispatched an army of occupation *before* he knew of Dewey's victory at Manila. That was before his famous night of prayer, during which the Lord reportedly advised him to annex the Philippines because it would be cowardly, unbusinesslike, and impolitic not to keep them.

These considerations were revealed with increasing candor as the United States went to war. On April 11, 1898, McKinley asked the Congress for army and navy forces "to secure a full and final termination of hostilities between the Government of Spain and the people of Cuba." Following his advice and request, the resulting Congressional action of April 19 did *not* recognize the revolutionary authorities in Cuba. McKinley signed the resolutions on April 20 and immediately demanded that Spain "at once relinquish its authority" in the island.

Spanish officials in the United States promptly advised their government of the obvious: "Consider war as declared." McKinley blockaded portions of the Cuban coast on April 22. Spain duly observed the formalities by declaring war two days later. Displaying considerably more candor than it did 63 years later, the Congress then made the American declaration of war retroactive to April 21. And in introducing his famous amendment against the annexation of Cuba, Senator Henry M. Teller offered a luminous insight into the whole affair. Americans would not take Cuba, he promised, "whatever we may do as to some other islands."[1]

---

1. Teller's morality and humanitarianism need not be questioned in order to note that he was also concerned in the case of Cuba to protect American beet sugar interests from tough competition.

The United States did reserve the right to intervene in Cuba when it decided that circumstances required such action "for the preservation of Cuban independence, [and] the maintenance of a government adequate for the protection of life, property, and individual liberty." Cubans were forced to incorporate this prerogative, already enacted into law by the American Congress, into their own Constitution. Availing itself of this sanction for intervention, the United States landed troops in 1906, 1912, and 1917. Cubans were convinced, after these episodes, that Washington intended to enforce its definition of an "adequate" government, and thereafter until 1961 the United States accomplished its purposes through the threat of force or the use of its vast economic power.

Benefiting from such strategic security, and even more from their own dominant position in the island, American interests quickly established themselves as the determining element in the Cuban economy. The United States thus defined and enforced limits on the political, economic, and social development of Cuba. To claim credit for the resulting benefits without acknowledging the tremendous imbalance of power, or without accepting responsibility for the unfavorable results, is at best to undertake a stupendous exercise in casuistry and at worst to engage in the most blatant kind of hypocrisy. Cuba had become part of the American empire.

It is true that Cubans generally acquiesced in this pattern of foreign control. The minority of the population that enjoyed direct connections with, and benefits from, American interests understandably favored the status quo. The majority also gained in a limited and sporadic way from American influence. But it is quite wrong to interpret such acquiescence, and the failure to sustain an overt, intense, and continuous anti-Americanism, as meaning either that the Cubans forgot about their inferior position or that they approved of the situation. Given the vast discrepancy of power between the United States and Cuba, such acquiescence represented the closest approximation to sanity that was possible under the circumstances. No nation can play the martyr continuously. Even so, the diplomatic records of the United States bear blunt and detailed witness to the way that "adequate" Cuban rulers, and policy-makers in Washington, constantly worried about the eruption of anti-imperialist feeling and about the possibilities of still another revolution.

These considerations are especially relevant in evaluating the Cuban policy of the United States after the election of President Franklin Delano Roosevelt. Combined with the inherent imbalance and inequities of its operations in Cuba, the American economic system's failure in 1929 generated a revolutionary crisis in Cuba. Quite in keeping with their own Good Neighbor policy, for which they are even yet given far too little credit, President Herbert Hoover and Secretary of State Henry L. Stimson refused to intervene as the government of Gerardo Machado began to lose control of the situation.

The Roosevelt New Deal administration changed all that. Concluding that Machado was unable to maintain a government "adequate" by American standards, and concerned lest a radical movement come to power, Secretary of State Cordell Hull and Ambassador Sumner Welles immediately launched a campaign to find or create a suitable replacement. Their broad objectives were to thwart the radicals, to restore law and order under conservative and amenable rulers, to protect American economic interests, to check Japanese economic competition, and (in Hull's words) to "open new markets for American farm and factory products."

Welles asked several times for at least a token garrison of marines to provide assistance in carrying out his end of the operation. Roosevelt and Hull opposed his requests on the grounds that such intervention should be avoided unless it became absolutely necessary because it would probably involve the United States in a prolonged occupation. In all other respects, however, the President and the Secretary supported a program of vigorous intervention. Their weapons included a

9

task force of between 30 and 40 ships of the United States Navy on station around Cuba, economic sanctions and the threat of even further pressure, promises of future aid if American wishes were followed, and the very considerable talents of Welles as a political middleman who finally constructed a conservative and reliable coalition government through prolonged negotiations and collaboration with Cuban army sergeant Fulgencio Batista.

Though they ultimately succeeded, American diplomats had tough going during the late summer and fall of 1933. The Cuban A.B.C. party, an organization composed of professional leaders, students, and their followers, became increasingly anti-American and antagonistic toward foreign investments. It initially provided vigorous support for the revolutionary government of Ramon Grau San Martin, which came to power in September, 1933. Grau's government, and its radical supporters, were firmly opposed by the Roosevelt administration.

To start with, Welles was upset because Grau's victory interrupted an apparently successful effort to secure "a practical monopoly of the Cuban market for American imports." He also feared for the future of American investments. Welles thought it "hardly likely" that Grau could form an "adequate" government, and set about to prove the accuracy of his estimate. He told Hull that the new government was "highly prejudicial to our interests," and stated flatly that "our own commercial and export interests cannot be revived under this government." Welles and his successor, Jefferson Caffery, shared an unfavorable attitude toward the "ignorant masses who have been misled by utopian promises." Both men, along with their superiors in Washington, preferred to deal with "the better classes"; even though, as Caffery lamented on one occasion, "the ignorant masses of Cuba reach a very high figure."

Roosevelt's refusal to recognize the Grau government gave Welles the freedom of maneuver that he needed in dealing with Batista and other conservative Cubans. Non-recognition was on the surface a restrained, passive action, but in reality it pushed Cuba around and around in a vicious circle. (It functions that way in connection with any poor and imbalanced society that is primarily dependent upon its economic relations with the United States.) Non-recognition effectively blocked Grau's ability to win acceptance by any other major power. That in turn increased the already tremendous economic and political pressure that the United States was exerting on Grau, and also subjected every Cuban to additional physical deprivation and psychological duress.

These effects of non-recognition raise a central question that both liberals and conservatives prefer to evade when discussing American foreign policy: Is it really so much more moral and humane to intimidate a society through the belly than to intimidate it at the point of a gun? Neither Roosevelt, Hull, nor Welles ever faced that question directly, but they apparently convinced themselves that intervention was mere meddling so long as marines were not used. In any event, the economic and psychological results of non-recognition increased and intensified the revolutionary fervor in Cuba. And that agitation, which included direct action against American property, was then used by the United States as further justification for non-recognition. Grau's generally effective action against such radicalism (it antagonized the A.B.C. party, for example) was dismissed by the United States as insufficient unto its need.

The Welles-Batista alliance finally defeated Grau. Roosevelt and Hull gave full support to the campaign. On October 4, 1933, Welles made a candid report to Hull about his collaboration with Batista that effectively summarizes the entire operation. "I told him that in my judgment he himself was the only individual in Cuba today who represented authority. . . . This I told him had rallied to his own support the very great majority of the commercial and financial interests in Cuba who are looking for protection." Welles remarked, as something of an afterthought, that the whole effort to undo a legitimate and functioning government through intrigue with a member of that government's armed forces was, "of course, anomalous." Indeed it was, but neither Hull nor Roosevelt called a halt to the subversion. On at least one occasion, moreover, Roosevelt knowingly made disingenuous and misleading remarks about the Welles operation at a press conference. The President seemed hugely to enjoy the game of make-believe.

Having imposed its will through the technique of controlling Cuban politics by means of a working agreement with the effective head of the Cuban army, the Roosevelt administration then generously surrendered its legal right to intervene with its own military forces. It also negotiated somewhat more favorable terms for Cuban sugar in the American market as part of a deal including commercial arrangements favoring American exports in the Cuban market. (This system took away with one hand some of what the New Deal was giving Americans with the other hand. Housewives paid an added increment of about five cents per ten-pound bag of sugar.) And, finally, the United States began to set up financial assistance for certain public works programs in Cuba.

These overtures of good will and sophisticated business strategy did not, unfortunately, put Cuba on the high road of balanced political and economic development. Hull's prompt and cordial recognition of the new government formally headed by Carlos Mendieta did not halt the "intense and prolonged" agitation inside Cuba about American intervention. Neither did it pinch off the general demand by Cubans for fundamental changes in their society. Mendieta suffered through two years of what he accurately described as "most grave problems of public order and a social disturbance."

The United States loyally supported Mendieta as he suspended habeas corpus and other constitutional guarantees, and used the army in March, 1935, to suppress a general strike. The situation was so unstable that even Batista was at one point worried enough to give Mendieta repeated warnings to organize a new cabinet that would have at least "some support among the public."

The most succinct estimate of New Deal intervention in the Cuban crises of the 1930's appears in Bryce Wood's study of *The Making of the Good Neighbor Policy*. "The pre-1930 social and economic class structure was retained, and the important place in the Cuban economy held by foreign enterprises was not fundamentally disturbed." The United States further consolidated Batista's position as arbiter of Cuban affairs through his official visit to Washington in November, 1938. Having been greeted upon his arrival by Welles, Batista then went on to important conferences with Roosevelt and Hull.

Within a year, however, the United States was again involved in difficulties in Cuba. The island's economy was in serious trouble by 1939, and the government continued in default of the public works loan and proposed to institute a mortgage moratorium. The United States protested vigorously against both measures, recalling in a somewhat arrogant redundancy that it had, "on frequent occasions," stressed the importance of Cuba maintaining a positive and friendly attitude toward the "very considerable investments of American capital" in the island.

The Cuban reply first emphasized the extreme difficulties in the island's economy. The mortgage moratorium, for example, was explained and defended as an effort to deal with an issue that touched "the very social and economic marrow of the country." The Cubans suggested that the American government, and the investors for which it spoke, might profitably accept short-run sacrifices in order to guarantee their long-range interests. Secretary Hull had indicated his belief in the wisdom of that approach in a memorandum on Cuban relations in 1934, but he did not act upon it in 1939.

Turning next to more general factors, the Cubans argued that they deserved some special consideration. For a long period of time, they noted, they had given Washington "singular cooperation" in support of American foreign policy. And in spite of strong natural emotions to the contrary, Cuba had permitted the United States to maintain "a very important" military base on its territory. Finally, the Cuban government warned American policy-makers that the United States was "frankly unpopular" among the majority of Cubans. That was not surprising, however, in view of American demands "of such onerous transcendency" made in the context of "such an adverse economic situation."

The Roosevelt administration was not even very sympathetic to the Cuban case, and it most certainly did not offer to work out a generous compromise. Hull instead read the Cubans his standard lecture on the importance of "orderly and stable governments," and on the "necessity of governments maintaining their obligations" in economic matters. The Secretary was at least candid: "The various agencies of our Government would find it impossible to cooperate with Cuba in a program of economic assistance until these obligations were met." It made no difference that Hull himself agreed that new public works were "much needed," or that the Secretary's advisors thought that "the development of any new productive facilities in Cuba" would be particularly desirable.

Hull did prove willing to provide some assistance once the Cubans stopped toying with radical measures, but the nature of his proposals only confirmed traditional American policy. Taken singly, and considered against the needs of the Cuban economy, the American projects were relevant and useful. For that matter, the Cubans shared the concern for a "thoroughgoing reorganization of the fiscal administration and reform of the tax system." Even conservatives had come to see the wisdom of paying part of their own way. The Cuban government also wanted funds for improving the Havana waterworks and for sanitation systems.

But the pattern of American proposals made it clear that the New Deal wanted to underwrite the rationalization of

14

American influence in Cuba. Hull saw the fiscal and tax program as "essential" to business expansion. He was particularly concerned, for example, with a form of "mineral taxation" that would facilitate American operations. The highways he recommended involved "certain tourist developments," and the need to "open up mineral resources."

In a similar way, the projected system of agricultural credit was designed to stabilize the existing sugar economy. Any diversification of agriculture was to involve "non-competitive products." And to cap its entire program, the United States demanded a new treaty "in order, particularly, to protect the status of citizens of the two countries residing in and doing business in the other country." It seems needless to belabor the point that Hull was not concerned about the safety of Cuban investments in the United States.

Conforming to their traditional role, the Cubans gave way and the American program sputtered into operation. But as with the United States itself, Cuban recovery from the depression came only with World War II. The gains which were then forthcoming included an increase in real per capita income due primarily to the quantitative growth of the existing economy, and to the commodity price increases, during the forced draft of the war and postwar crises. There was also a modest qualitative improvement in the functioning of the established economic system. But there were no significant changes in the social and political structure beyond the fact that Batista's personal rule became increasingly tyrannical. Adolf A. Berle, Jr's. estimate of the situation is essentially correct: "great luxury for a relatively small group in Havana and a small rise above the starvation level for the masses."

This summary review of the years 1895-1959 suggests that several features of American-Cuban relations exercised a pervasive influence on the nature and development of Castro's Revolution:

(1) American military, political, and economic power was employed throughout the period to set limits upon, and control, the economic, social, and political development of Cuba.

(2) American power was consistently deployed and used to support conservative and even reactionary Cuban governments that thwarted or repressed any and all efforts to effect fundamental social and economic changes.

(3) From the very beginning, when the United States refused in 1898 to recognize and deal with the revolutionary government in Cuba, the exercise of American power created and sustained a growing anti-Americanism. Due to the length and the nature of American predominance, that antagonism had by the end of World War II become far more pervasive than the anti-Americanism in any other Latin American country during the 20th century with the sole (but revealing) exception of the feeling that existed in Mexico between 1910 and 1941. The Mexican analogy is particularly illuminating, not only because American holdings in agriculture, oil, mining, and trade were involved in both cases, but because Cuba's Revolution of 1959 was clearly influenced by the Mexican example and has in some respects developed along similar lines.

(4) Finally, the Mexican example dramatizes the extensive American responsibility as of January 1, 1959, to initiate actions toward Cuba that would demonstrate that the United States finally meant to behave in keeping with its professed ideals and promises. The United States had ultimately made that kind of adjustment in its dealings with Mexico. The lesson had been learned, however, only at great human and economic cost to Americans and Mexicans alike.

Even so, the experience was not applied to the Cuban situation. That unhappy failure does not, however, absolve the United States of its great and primary responsibility in connection with the Cuban Revolution. For even if one argues that Cuba was lost the minute Castro came to power—and that

16

interpretation is not actually tenable—the United States still had the responsibility to retreat from the island with graciousness and dignity. Great Britain moved with some considerable dignity, even majesty, during its withdrawal from India, and the United States could have matched that performance.

A Revolution to Build a New Nation and a New Epoch

Even the first newspaper accounts of the triumph of the Castro Revolution stressed the intensity and fervor of the upheaval against Batista. A deep feeling and spirit of being against more than just Batista, and of being for a new order in Cuba, permeated the entire population as it converged on Havana to celebrate the victory. Draper seriously overstates the case when he says that the Cuban middle class was "ready for deep-going social and political reforms," but in the first flush of the triumph a good many members of that class at least *thought* they were ready for that kind of change.

Nationalism, anti-imperialism, and the urge to social reform converged in Cuba in 1958 and 1959 in much the same way as they had done in other dependent or colonial societies ever since the end of World War II. The casual American image of Cuba as a combination of Go-Go-Go baseball players, spinning roulette wheels, and racy women set off against a pleasing background of handsome and efficient businessmen, quaint but noble and manly farmers, and a sensual sunset is considerably less than helpful in understanding the Revolution and its evolution. It is essential to realize that Cuba was a society of desperate contrasts and staggering contradictions struggling to break finally free of the limitations of an unbalanced and lurching economy.

Though they devote far less space to the problem than Draper does, Meyer and Szulc provide a generally more useful insight into Cuba's political economy on the eve of Castro's triumph. It is not sociologically precise, but then neither is Draper's, and they at least reveal the mood and feel of the situation with power and vividness. The American-Cuban relationship, "scarcely healthy," had produced "a composite of West Germany and Egypt, affluence and harsh feudal poverty side by side." They boldly invoke the image of 19th century empire to describe the milieu of Cuba's upper class: "It was colonial life at its feudal, opulent and amusing best."

Draper will have none of that kind of talk. He first says that Cuba had "serious social problems, but it was far from being a peasant country or even a typically 'underdeveloped' one." Since the careful study by Paul G. Hoffman, *One Hundred Countries,* ranks Cuba just within the top 10 percent of the underdeveloped countries, it would seem fair enough to describe Cuba as being a relatively rich underdeveloped country blocked from further improvement of a significant nature. But to say that it is "far" from being typically underdeveloped is simply inaccurate.

Draper offers various per capita (and other) statistics to support his description. He notes, for example, that Cuba before Castro was "an *exporter* of meat." He apparently means to suggest or imply, or even to prove, the existence of a surplus beyond the minimum needs of the population. The fact, though true, can carry no such load of interpretation. It merely establishes that American and Cuban ranchers and farmers exported meat that other Cubans could not afford to buy. Export statistics are in themselves a notoriously inaccurate guide to the level of balanced economic development. And though they are somewhat more useful, per capita figures are also very misleading unless correlated with other data.

Draper's difficulty with statistics is nicely illustrated by his report on American military aid to Batista's Cuba after 1945. Comparing the totals for several Latin American countries and correlating the figures with population data, he concludes that the assistance was "relatively modest." But military-aid operations involve not only the level of existing strength and the security estimate for the country, but also the amount of military space that is to be protected. To consider only the last point, geographic areas, Batista's $10.6 millions turns out to be much more than "relatively modest." On the basis of dollars per square mile of responsibility, Batista received the second highest amount of aid given to the nations that Draper uses for his comparison. In any event, Draper remarks a bit later that Batista's army "had for years obtained as much arms as it had wanted from the United States and other countries."

In substantiating his original description of the Cuban economy, Draper points out that only Venezuela, Argentina, and Chile of Latin American countries enjoyed a higher per capita income. He adds that 57 percent of the population was urban, and that only 40 percent of the people drew their living from the land. He does not explain, however, whether this includes city dwellers who earn their living from sugar and other agrarian operations. Neither does he mention a good many other statistics that are at least as important as those he chooses to reproduce.

Draper does not tell us, for example, that infant mortality in Cuba was the fourth highest in Latin America in 1940. Nor do we learn from him that manufacturing in Cuba employed only 14.2 percent of the labor force in 1943, while the trade and service sectors accounted for 44 percent. Or that sugar yield per acre actually declined from 17.4 metric tons before the war to 15.5 in 1948. Neither does he mention that in 1955-1956 a mere 8 percent of Cuban farms accounted for almost 75 percent of the land (one-half of one percent controlled more than 33 percent), while 69.7 percent of the farms held but 11.2 percent of the land, and that some 200,000 families in agriculture had *no* land.

American investment in Cuba is another subject that Draper does not mention. But Americans controlled 80 percent of the utilities, 90 percent of the mines, 90 percent of the cattle ranches, almost 100 percent of the oil refining industry, 50 percent of the public railways, 40 percent of the sugar industry,

21

and 25 percent of all bank deposits. Cuba ranked fourth in Latin American per capita income and third in American investments. In addition, American firms took 40 percent of the profits on sugar, and their total earnings on direct investments amounted to $77 million (1957). On the other hand, these American companies employed but 1.08 percent of the Cuban population.[1]

Despite his initial remark about Cuba being "far" from typically underdeveloped, Draper finally points out that the economy of the island suffered from two features that are central to any definition of underdevelopment. First, it "was precariously dependent on the fluctuations of a single crop, sugar, which accounted for more than 80 percent of Cuban exports and employed about a half million workers for only three to four months a year." Second, "the social development of Cuba was shockingly unbalanced in favor of the cities and the towns." In the end, however, Draper settles for a description that blurs and confuses even that analysis. "Cuba was, in fact," he concludes, "an unevenly developed country with a relatively high standard of living."

The key word in that definition is of course *relative*. Draper offers two external bases for comparison. One is the concept of underdevelopment per se, and by that standard Cuba is underdeveloped. Indeed, he seems to miss the point that the great discrepancy between Cuba's potential and its actuality is one of the most devastating of all criticisms of American policy. The other scale is per capita income, and by that criterion Cuba is also underdeveloped. Judged by internal conditions, his assertion that the Cuban people enjoyed a "relatively high standard of living" is contradicted by his own admission of shocking extremes. A standard of living must include the condition of all those who live—however poorly they manage.

---

1. On this point see: Donald Villarejo, "American Investment in Cuba," *New University Thought*, Vol. I, No. 1 (Spring, 1960), 79-89.

It is true, however, that Draper's evaluation of the Cuban political economy jibes nicely with the three essential features of his interpretation of the Castro Revolution. American policy "was not the causative, operative factor," it "was essentially a middle class revolution," and "the revolution Castro promised was unquestionably betrayed." Before comparing that analysis with the one offered by Meyer and Szulc, and evaluating both of them against the evidence, it may be well to digress briefly to review the way that Draper judges other analysts of the Revolution. This seems particularly useful because of the considerable reputation and influence Draper has accumulated as an interpreter of the Revolution.

Draper is particularly critical, even disdainful, of those who describe the upheaval as a peasant revolution. He calls this idea "one of the first and favorite myths." The only trouble is that Draper drastically oversimplifies what other people actually said in order to attack them as mythmakers. Consider, for example, his judgment of the book, *Cuba: Anatomy of a Revolution,* written by Leo Huberman and Paul M. Sweezy. Even considering that it was prepared during the first half of 1960, their analysis and interpretation has several important weaknesses;[1] but the Draper point about their myth of a peasant revolution does not stand up under examination.

Huberman and Sweezy make three points in connection with the peasants: first, that the Castro leadership identified with the peasant problem and won active peasant support; second, that Castro's army was basically made up of, and largely supplied by, the peasants; and, third, that "in the two-year period from Christmas, 1956 . . . January 1, 1959, nearly all classes of the population had identified themselves, in varying degrees, with the July 26th Movement."

Either implicitly or explicitly, Draper makes and uses all

---

1. For example, they ignore the Constitution of 1940, and their discussion of the role of the labor movement in the Revolution is very scanty.

of those points in his own analysis. Hence his failure to call the reader's attention to the Huberman-Sweezy remark about "nearly all classes" is quite noticeable. What seems to bother Draper most about Huberman and Sweezy (other than his ideological differences with them) is the way that they discuss the peasants as a revolutionary force. He does not deny, however, that the peasants backed Castro and his original July 26th Movement in the first two ways they describe. Nor can he. They did. They also supported him after the victory over Batista.

The only additional comment that seems necessary involves the way that Draper discounts the role of Castro's small army in the triumph over Batista. Contrary to what Draper implies, Batista would not have collapsed if that army—small as it was—had not existed and fought engagements with the regulars. That tiny force served not only as a rallying point for other groups, but did in battle demonstrate and dramatize the collapse of the former sergeant's control of the Cuban Army.

Draper is critical but contradictory in his judgment of the work of the late C. Wright Mills, *Listen, Yankee!* He first says that "the Castro leaders talked in much the way Mills recorded them. Sometimes the words in the book were so close to those I had heard that I felt I knew the name of the source. . . . I consider those long monologues more or less authentic." A bit later, however, Draper complains of the Cubans that Mills has presented that "one never knows where they end and he begins." Further on, though, Draper is once again very sure where Mills stops and the Cubans begin. Part of this unevenness probably results from Draper's failure to write a book instead of just reprinting three magazine articles, but he had plenty of time to revise and add new material where he chose to do so, and hence the contradictions and ambiguities that remain must be taken as indicative of Draper's work on the Revolution.

Draper also criticizes Mills quite sharply for not writing a better book. (He does this through one of his favorite devices, the grand rhetorical question that goes unanswered on the implicit grounds that the reply is obvious to all but the perverse. This may be a technique appropriate to winning minor points in a debate, but it is out of place in serious analysis.) Actually, Draper himself could have been much more helpful if he had made up his own mind on Mills's Cubans, and then specified which of the monologues he considered particularly useful. One may add in conclusion that Draper might also have been more generous to Jean Paul Sartre. For, despite his critical comments on the Frenchman's book (*Sartre On Cuba*), Draper uses the same analysis about the Castro Revolution having no ideology.

Thus refreshed by a tipple of skepticism about the pattern of judgments he provides, let us return to Draper's own—and in some ways impressive—interpretation of Castro's Revolution. American policy "was not the causative, operative factor," it "was essentially a middle class revolution," and "the revolution Castro promised was unquestionably betrayed."

Alongside of this let us next set down the main features of the Meyer-Szulc interpretation. For betrayal, read tragedy. "The history of the Cuban Revolution has an air of inevitability about it in the grand manner of classical tragedy, in which the myriad actors seem fated to perform their assigned roles although they know the drama is bound to end in calamity." For middle-class revolution read a more radical movement lacking a clear set of ideas and hence willfully using a forced and artificial anti-Americanism as its ideological guideline.

Finally, in place of Draper's denial of American policy as the causative factor, read a curious ambivalence on the issue. On the one hand, American policy did influence events, and a different policy might—there is, they say, "a great body of evidence"—have influenced "an obviously hesitant" Castro and thereby produced much less harmful results.[1] On the other hand, it was inevitable that the United States would act as it did, and also certain that nothing could have altered Castro's willful anti-Americanism.

Time after time, Meyer and Szulc fall back on the model of classic tragedy to resolve the contradiction in their analysis. Their explanation of the inevitability nevertheless offers a crucial insight into the whole question of American influence. The course of events was inevitable, they say, "because the United States government and much American public opinion, including segments of the press, had not fully perceived the depth of the Cuban Revolution." It was in reality a "transfiguring emotional experience. . . . Release of pent-up feelings of frustration . . . overwhelming welling up of pride . . . a dizzying sense of participation in building a new nation and a new epoch." Draper agrees: the Cuban upheaval was "a genuine revolution."

Meyer and Szulc admit, moreover, that the American reaction to this stirring social revolution, "more often than not, was dry, legalistic and phlegmatic." They add something that is even more revealing: "The invasion plan was in some sense a logical extension of prevailing attitudes to a revolutionary situation."

---

1. An incidental but nevertheless serious criticism of their book is that they never present any of this "great body of evidence."

3

America's Greeting to the Revolution

Draper's proposition about the relationship between American policy and the Castro Revolution is unhelpful because it is too forced, artificial, and brittle. It will not even serve as a viable hypothesis with which to examine the data. There is a vast and terribly misleading oversimplification involved in saying, as he does, that American policy was not *"the"* causative factor in the development of the Cuban Revolution. If one wants to discuss the matter in that black and white manner, then Adolf A. Berle's judgment is far more accurate. The Cuban situation, he wrote in 1960, "inescapably reflects a failure of American foreign policy."

In the first place, a phenomenon of the size, complexity, and intensity of Castro's Revolution cannot, given the history of the island's 63-year American tutelage, be isolated and discussed as a self-contained episode. Secondly, there was not merely one American policy as is implied in Draper's remark. At the very least, there were two American policies that have to be evaluated for their causative influence on Cuban developments. One was the American policy from 1895 to 1959, and more especially from 1933 to 1959. The other was American policy after Castro toppled Batista.

American policy prior to 1959 is initially noted, then misconceived and underestimated in its impact, and then implicitly discounted by Meyer and Szulc. Draper ignores it, save for a few remarks the tone of which discount its influence. Early in their book, Meyer and Szulc refer to "the tremendous potential of Cuban resentment against the United States government." Much later, they again comment on this anti-Americanism and describe it as a "reflex born of their experience in living on an island where the United States traditionally had the final say."

Despite these perceptive remarks, the basic Meyer-Szulc argument flatly asserts that the Revolution "could have pursued its goals in a democratic fashion with at least the passive acquiescence of Washington . . . if the leaders in Havana had not been determined to confirm their darkest suspicions about Yankee imperialism." They go so far as to say that the United States followed a "policy of patience and forebearance." The causal relevance and significance of the traditional pattern of American control and the reflex it produced are thus dropped in favor of the assertion that Castro made an "early decision to portray Cuba as a victim of American imperialism."

Meyer and Szulc argue that Castro had a choice: he could "allow this natural resentment to run its course—as was done in the South American countries where military dictatorships favored by Washington were overthrown," or he could "feed, exploit and build up popular passion by making anti-Americanism a basic theme of his regime."

The first thing to be said about all of this is crucial: Castro's Revolution was not just another South American revolt. The only comparable Latin American upheaval in the 20th century was the Mexican Revolution. That lasted from 1910 to 1941, and was characterized in each of its militant phases by a vigorous anti-Americanism. Hence to talk about Castro having a choice as though he were a man going out on the town for an evening on an executive vice-president's expense account is to speak of some fantasy world.

The baffling thing—baffling because it is so obviously contradictory—is that Meyer and Szulc (and Draper, too) stress the profound drive for change that characterized the Cuban Revolution. It is very difficult to understand, let alone accept, their argument. They write at one moment about Cubans giving vent to "pent-up frustrations . . . an overwhelming welling up of pride," and being motivated by an urge to build a "new nation and a new epoch," and in the next minute make assertions about letting one of the most natural manifestations of those feelings run its course.

Either the Revolution was a "transfiguring emotional experience" or it was not. By all accounts it was, and that means one of two things. It means either that Castro and his associates were very jumpy, on historical as well as psychological grounds, about the American reaction to the Revolution. Or it means that they realized very clearly that nobody could build "a new nation and a new epoch" in Cuba without disrupting the existing pattern of American control.

In the first case, the reactions of Castro that Meyer and Szulc make so much of become understandable without any reference to willful campaigns against the United States. If the second alternative is correct, then Castro knew the Revolution was certain to become involved in a situation fraught with great tension, and possibly even intervention and defeat. He would very naturally—and properly, too, for that matter— have been on the lookout for any signs of developing American policy. He would also have been very apt, particularly in view of Washington's support for Batista, to overestimate any unfavorable indicators.

These two interpretations have been discussed separately in order to clarify the alternatives to the Meyer-Szulc approach. The evidence, as well as what we know in general about human action, suggests that Castro's behavior was produced by a mixture of both attitudes. Known to be a man whose emotions ran close to his tongue, he was also very excited and noticeably weary in the hour of victory. Nor was there any opportunity for him to get away, relax, and take the long view during the next few weeks. And the only kind of revolutionary leader who would not have been intensely concerned with the American attitude would have been a conservative who assumed an identity of interests between himself and the United States.

Meyer and Szulc do not explore these alternatives that

are available for explaining Castro's action. Instead, they assert that "it seems evident that Castro was determined" to be anti-American. "Castro launched his anti-Yankee campaign, subtly at first, and then more and more openly and blatantly, months before the Agrarian Reform Law went into effect." Their argument is very feeble. For one thing, they keep right on talking about Castro's indecision and ambivalence concerning relations with the United States.

In a more specific way, Meyer and Szulc make a great deal, in their efforts to establish Castro's willful anti-Americanism at a very early date, of a speech that they say Castro delivered before a luncheon group at the Havana Rotary Club on January 13, 1959. The episode turns up several times in their book. The more they talk about it, however, the less it seems to support their first and basic interpretation. This analysis and charge is as follows: Castro's anti-American "campaign was insinuatingly begun on January 13."

They offer two pieces of evidence in support of this interpretation. They report that, on his way to the luncheon, Castro made what even they refer to as an "impulsive" remark about "200,000 gringos" dying if the United States intervened with force. Then, with reference to the speech itself, they note that Castro "pointedly reminded his audience that Cuba had always been governed by foreigners." "Cuba was not free," Castro explained, "because when a foreigner arrogates for himself the right of intervening in the affairs of a country, that country is not free." Meyer and Szulc admit that this observation was "palpably true" in connection with American-Cuban relations. They nevertheless stick to their interpretation of Castro's remarks as proof of willful and unjustified anti-Americanism. They give as their reason that it was made "in the opening days of the revolution at the very moment when the United States was casting about for ways of embracing the Cuban revolution with belated tenderness."

It is difficult to take this argument with any seriousness

30

whatsoever. Nor would there be any reason to do so were it not that Meyer and Szulc, Draper, other commentators who follow their basic thesis, and the United States government itself have insisted on this general line of interpretation with such persistence and success that large numbers of people seem now convinced that Castro's anti-Americanism had little, if any, basis in fact, and that American policy had almost nothing to do with the development of the Cuban Revolution. That being the case, it becomes necessary to examine this charge of a willful and unjustified anti-American campaign being "insinuatingly" started on January 13.

It may be noted at the outset that the one thing to bet on two weeks after Batista's downfall would have been that the triumphant revolutionary leader would talk about American complicity in Cuba's troubles. It would be extremely difficult, even with considerable thought, to come up with a more probable proposition. The further one examines the Meyer-Szulc assertion, moreover, the less one is persuaded of its validity.

But let us assume, at least to begin with, that Meyer and Szulc are correct in their report of what happened on January 13, 1959. Many pages later in their book, they add a rather interesting bit of information about the events of that day. They reveal that Castro had been attacked on January 12 by Senator Wayne Morse. They explain that the Senator called the court martial trials and executions of Batista lieutenants and accomplices a "blood bath."

An examination of the Senator's remarks reveals (as might have been expected by anyone at all familiar with his record) that Morse used more words than that. The ones omitted by Meyer and Szulc are quite important. Morse announced from the floor of the Senate on January 12 that he was "horror stricken by the new blood bath in Cuba," and referred to the manifestations of "great concern" that had already been made by others in the United States. He next pointedly mentioned his position as Chairman of the Senate Subcommittee on Latin

31

American Affairs. Then he "deplored" the situation in Cuba and added that he had interrupted the Senate in its struggle over limiting the practice of filibusters "to give this word of warning to the officials of the new Cuban Government. Killing their opponents is not the way . . . to win the support of free men and women around the world."

Now whatever Americans may think of Senator Morse and his bipartisan wanderings in search of a haven congenial to his particular brand of liberalism, the Cubans could hardly be expected to discount his remarks. He was, after all, just what he said he was: Chairman of the Senate Subcommittee on Latin American Affairs. And given their knowledge of New Deal diplomacy toward Cuba in the revolutionary situation of 1933-1934, it is not unlikely that Cuban leaders had another reaction. It seems rather probable that they interpreted Morse's performance as a striking example of the crusading American liberal who raised his hands and voice in outrage, and his influence in opposition, when the analyses, criticisms, and reforms he advocated were taken seriously by leaders of a revolution in an underdeveloped country.

In and of themselves, those considerations would seem more than sufficient to account for Castro's remarks about the United States on the following day, January 13. But, and still accepting the Meyer-Szulc account of what happened on January 13, it is also necessary to remember that reporters in the lobby of the Havana Hilton Hotel "needled" Castro about Morse (and other American critics such as the *Washington Post*) as he was on his way to the luncheon at the Rotary Club. Less mercurial figures than Castro have been known to respond in kind under those circumstances.

Even that is not all. Meyer and Szulc do not mention it, but it was common knowledge in January that the United States was sending marines to Haiti in an effort to help strongman François Duvalier engineer a modest relaxation of his dictatorial rule. The marines were assigned the specific job of reorganizing and training Duvalier's army and police force. Castro and other Cuban leaders could hardly interpret the action in any way save as another Operation Batista. And, in addition, Haitian opponents of Duvalier were using Cuba as a sanctuary.

It was also well known in January that the United States had demanded very stiff conditions in its negotiations with Argentina for a loan. It was also understood that the loan was not unconnected with Argentina's agreement to allow American oil companies to expand their operations. By the middle of January, moreover, it was being reported that the cost of living in Argentina had jumped between 15 and 20 percent as the result of the requirements insisted upon by the United States in return for the loan, and the country was torn by strikes and other protest demonstrations. This was the first of the so-called "stabilization loans," and the provisions established by American officials caused very prompt and painful consequences in Argentina. And in January, President Arturo Frondizi found it wise to take special security precautions as he left the airport on a trip to discuss such difficulties in the United States.

There is still more background for what Meyer and Szulc present as Castro's Rotary Club speech on January 13, even though they again fail to review such matters. Castro had told the Eisenhower administration on August 26, 1958, that America's continued military assistance to Batista "produces deep resentment." The State Department's belated reply repeated the usual catechism about non-intervention, even though a Department official admitted that aid from the United States was "certainly" being used "to beat back" the revolutionary forces. That episode was topped by the appearance of Secretary of State John Foster Dulles (at that time a very sick man) at a Cuban Embassy reception only two days before Batista made a mockery of the election of November 2, 1958.

Dulles not only drank a toast to the Batista government

that inglorious evening, but appears to have given his verbal approval to a last minute move to keep Castro from coming to power.[1] William D. Pawley, a former diplomat who knew Batista, says he proposed the plan during the first week of December, 1958, in an after-dinner conversation with officials of the Department of State and the Central Intelligence Agency.

As he later explained it in sworn testimony, Pawley's idea was to persuade Batista "to capitulate to a caretaker government unfriendly to him but satisfactory to us, which we could immediately recognize and give military assistance to in order that Fidel Castro not come to power." Undersecretary of State C. Douglas Dillon appears to have cleared the proposal through to Dulles, who apparently approved it over the telephone. Pawley testified that he flew to Havana to see Batista and "spent 3 hours with him on the night of December 9." Batista refused the offer, but it may be presumed that Castro either knew of the maneuver at the time it took place, or that he found out about it soon thereafter. Whatever definition one chooses to use, this was certainly an overt American act against Castro.

The end is not yet. On January 2, 1959, American officials allowed newspapers to refer to their "apprehension" about Cuba's future under Castro. Various American business interests were also reported to be antagonistic. And the accredited American Ambassador, Earl T. Smith, who was trade-marked by his connections with Batista, stayed on at his post until January 10, 1959. Meyer and Szulc nevertheless assert that the United States was by January 13 "casting about for ways of embracing the Cuban revolution with belated tenderness." They do not commit themselves as to when the search began. But the United

---

1. Draper does not mention this episode. Neither do Meyer and Szulc. A short account is provided by one of the men who served in the revolutionary government: Rivero, *Castro's Cuba*. The primary evidence is in *Communist Threat to the United States Through the Caribbean. Hearings before the Sub-Committee* [of the Senate Judiciary Committee] *to Investigate the Administration of the Internal Security Act and Other Internal Security Laws,* Part 10 (Washington: G.P.O., 1961).

States did not recognize Cuba's new government until January 7, and it does not seem that it would have been beyond the realm of decorum for Washington to send a special emissary with the note.

It is true that the man who finally replaced Smith, Philip W. Bonsal, was a career officer who had performed well in Colombia and Bolivia. There is reason to doubt, however, whether that experience prepared him for handling relations with a deeply revolutionary government. It hardly seems likely, in this connection, that a career diplomat specializing in Latin American affairs would need six weeks to prepare himself for the job. If he did, then he was not the man for the task. But that is how long it took him to reach Havana. He was not even appointed until January 21, and did not arrive in Havana until February 19, 1959. The United States had no ambassador in Cuba during that crucial period of the Revolution. It may be that the Embassy staff provided excellent reports, but the Cuban government no doubt interpreted the situation in a different light.

Castro nevertheless used the resignation of Smith on January 10 as the opportunity to offer a generous gesture. "I am under the impression," he said publicly and for quotation, "that the United States is changing its attitude toward Cuba and will remove the things that caused friction [in the past], but that is for the United States to say." The more one studies the evidence, the more one is persuaded that Castro's remark of January 10 provides an important clue to subsequent relations between America and Cuba.

It clearly indicated a willingness on the part of Castro to modify past feelings on the basis of new evidence. But it also revealed a very straightforward placing of the primary responsibility for such improvements on the United States. Now by any standard of equity, that is where the responsibility belonged. But that is precisely what neither American policymakers, nor most American commentators on the Revolution, have proved willing to acknowledge and act upon. They have instead, and as typified by Meyer and Szulc, shifted the responsibility to Castro and Cuba.

Up to this point, the Meyer-Szulc interpretation of Castro's speech of January 13 has been examined on the assumption that their account is accurate, at least insofar as they present the information they offer in an authentic manner. We have seen, of course, that they do not tell all the significant things about even the Morse attack of January 12, let alone reporting other salient aspects of the context of Castro's remarks. But even on their terms, their charge that Castro "insinuatingly" started a willful campaign of anti-Americanism is not supported by the evidence.

The facts of the case are that Castro's anti-American comments of January 13, 1959, would have been an inherent part of any fundamental revolution in Cuba, that they were both explicable and understandable in view of the character of American overlordship during the preceding 63 years, and that neither Senator Morse nor other officials in the United States had greeted the Cuban Revolution in a way that promised an easing of that tension.

These points become even more dramatic when it is realized that *Meyer and Szulc are factually wrong in their account of Castro's speech on January 13, 1959.*

Now every historian makes factual mistakes. Most of them are accidental and also incidental. Very few such errors actually demolish an argument or destroy an interpretation.

Let us therefore have no misunderstanding about the first point being made here. It is assumed that Meyer and Szulc made the error quite accidentally.

It does not in this instance follow, however, that their error is also inconsequential. Indeed not. The mistakes involved in their account of Castro's January 13 speech serve to demolish the entire argument they develop around that event. Furthermore, a straight account of the episode serves to establish that the United States knowingly acted to bring pressure on the Castro government even though it had formally recognized it.

Castro did not give any speech before the Havana Rotary Club on January 13. He spoke that day before the Havana Lambs Club. He did in his remarks reply firmly, but without any outburst about marines, to the attack delivered by Senator Morse on January 12.

Castro did not address the Havana Rotary Club until January 15. With the record finally set straight, let us see if anything happened in connection with American policy on January 14, 1959, that might account for Castro's outburst. The diplomatic events of January 14 began when Secretary of State Dulles appeared before the Senate Foreign Relations Committee to give testimony lasting two hours. He spoke primarily about the Berlin crisis and other aspects of relations with Russia. But finally, at the very end of the session, Senator Morse raised the Cuban issue. He was "very much disturbed." Dulles sympathized. The Secretary wanted "a government of law and order and justice" in Cuba. Then there was an exchange of which the transcript reveals, despite part of it being deleted for publication purposes, that Dulles indicated that some kind of pressure on Castro was being given "very careful consideration."

This reading and extrapolation of the transcript of January 14 was formally and publicly verified on January 15. On that day, Morse and other Congressmen had a special session with Roy R. Rubottom, State Department advisor on Latin American affairs. A report leaked to the press revealed that the action Dulles had spoken of (off the record) on January 14 involved rushing a new Ambassador to Cuba in order to follow up on Morse's attack of January 12. It was finally decided, however, that a delay in sending an Ambassador would be more effective. This episode establishes beyond any question that the long delay in replacing Smith with Bonsal involved an official move to show displeasure with the new Cuban government.

Now Castro may not have learned about the Rubottom-Morse meeting of January 15 before he started to the Rotary Club luncheon on that day, although it is possible that the reporters who "needled" him included that tid-bit in their teasing. It would be helpful to know about this point, but it is not essential to an understanding of Castro's remark about the marines and the possibility of American intervention. The reason for this is that Morse did know, as a result of his off-the-record conversation with Dulles, what the Department had in mind by noon on January 14.

After his own lunch on that day, therefore, Morse went back to the Senate and resumed his attack of January 12. He began by noting that those earlier remarks had provoked a reply from the Cubans. This of course pleased him. He nevertheless dismissed the answer as a "fallacious rationalization." He then offered the following advice: "What Castro and Agramonte ought to do is drop on their knees before their Maker and ask for forgiveness." This time Morse won distinguished support in the Senate. Senator William J. Fulbright described the trials of Batista lieutenants as "deplorable" and identified himself with Morse's criticism.

It is now apparent that Meyer and Szulc seriously confuse and distort the entire background of Castro's remarks both before and after his lunch at the Havana Rotary Club on January 15, 1959. They proceed to make another error of omission that only adds to the muddle they have made of the story. *Castro almost immediately apologized for, and withdrew, his off-hand remark to the American reporters who had needled him.* Meyer and Szulc do not even mention the apology.

On the next day, January 16, 1959, Castro received some support in the Congress. Representative Adam Clayton Powell of New York asked his colleagues and other Americans to show some patience and sympathy with the Revolution. To make his point, he spread upon the record a full account of American aid to Batista. Representative Charles O. Porter of Oregon like-

38

wise advised restraint, but closed his remarks with the suggestion that the Inter-American Bar Association should send a
delegation to Havana to make sure that the Cuban trials were
not blood baths.

The majority of Congressmen was militantly critical. Representative Wayne L. Hays called for a proscription of tourist
travel to the island; if that did not coerce Castro sufficiently,
then he was ready for a trade embargo. Representative Em-
manuel Celler of Brooklyn proposed that the issue of the Cuban
trials be taken before the United Nations. That particular suggestion was applauded. Then Representative Victor L. Anfuso
of New York blandly asserted that "Castro is no better than
Batista." Castro "would do well," Anfuso explained, "to study
the map of the Western Hemisphere and learn the facts of
life, particularly as they affect the economy of his country."

"We will not stand for a Nasser or a Hitler so close to our
shores," Anfuso cried. "We demand respect from him." He
then made a direct threat. Castro had to change, otherwise "I
shall be the first to move before the House Committee on Agriculture, of which I am a member, and before the Congress of
the United States, to drastically reduce the sugar quota for
Cuba."

American leaders were not in a mood to heed even the
advice of Puerto Rican Governor Luis Muñoz Marin. The
Governor might have anticipated more influence. After all, he
had played a key role in the progress of Puerto Rico, and the
United States often pointed to the development of that island
as an example of what it was willing and able to do for underdeveloped countries. Muñoz Marin warned on January 19 that
the United States should demonstrate "the friendliest feelings"
and "the greatest possible forbearance" toward the Cuban
Revolution. Any other action would be self-defeating, even
dangerous.

The Governor was at least indirectly answered on January
20. Senator George Smathers of Florida entered the discussion,

39

referring at the outset of his remarks to the threats of economic intervention that had been made on several occasions. On the grounds that it had "acted with proper restraint" in deciding such matters, he praised the Department of State. He then announced that he was refusing a Cuban invitation to observe one of the court martial trials. Morse rose to reveal that he, too, had been invited but was likewise declining the offer. "We want to be friends," Morse explained, but first Castro had "to demonstrate to all of us" that he was fit to rule. Following the lead of his senior Democratic colleague Senator Fulbright, the liberal Senator Hubert Humphrey then joined the chorus. He praised Morse "for the quality of statesmanship and vision that he has demonstrated ever since the success of the Cuban Revolution."

It would also seem very probable that the Cubans, along with other nations in the world, kept a close eye on the official American reaction to the January, 1959, visit of Anastas I. Mikoyan to the United States. If they did not, they missed several important clues to the nature of basic American policy toward any revolutionary government. Perhaps the American response is the kind of thing that Meyer and Szulc had in mind when they later wrote that the invasion of Cuba was "in some sense a logical extension of prevailing attitudes to a revolutionary situation."

The American posture was negative. Secretary Dulles had a special word of praise for the labor leaders who "really stood up to" Mikoyan. That was "far sounder in the national interests" than any other course. C. Douglas Dillon, Under-Secretary of State for Economic Affairs, was even more candid about the way the United States handled the Russian's concern for more trade between the two countries.

Mikoyan argued that trade was good for politics. He explained, however, that the United States would have "to repeal the ban on most-favored-treatment for the Soviet Union," and "make available very large credits," before such trade could develop. "He said it was just nonsense," Dillon reported to the Congress, "to talk about trade if we didn't give the U.S.S.R. credits because obviously the Soviet Union was not in a position to balance its trade right away."

Dillon told Mikoyan that increased trade was out of the question unless and until the Soviet Union met certain conditions set by the United States. Russia would have to: (1) settle all outstanding debts, (2) "permit greater access by American companies to producing and consuming units within the Soviet Union," and (3) provide "assurances to foreigners of genuine protection for private industrial rights." The Cubans may of course have missed the enumeration of such demands by Dillon in January, 1959. But they were in any event familiar with the approach from Cuba's own experience in dealing with the United States, and were unquestionably concerned to avoid entrapping their own Revolution in such traditional arrangements.

All of these considerations, from the earlier relations with the United States through the events of January, 1959, make it clear that the policy of the United States did play a causative role in the development of the Cuban Revolution. Specifically, Morse's speech of January 12 provoked and disturbed the Cuban government and touched off a series of threats from American leaders in and out of the Congress. Up to that hour, and afterward throughout January, the influence of the United States was almost wholly negative. It served neither to encourage the Cubans to think that Washington would help them build "a new nation and a new epoch" nor even to reassure them that their own efforts would be tolerated. These events of January, 1959, upset and worried Castro. He candidly admitted, near the end of the month, that his estimate of January 10—"I am under the impression that the United States is changing its attitude toward Cuba"—might have been wrong.

The first instance in which American policy-makers suggested other, more favorable, possibilities came during Castro's visit to the United States in April, 1959. By that time, however,

Castro and the original July 26th Movement (and the coalition of other groups that supported them) had confronted their essential choice—were they, or were they not, going to return to the Constitution of 1940?

4

The Nature and Outlook of the
Original July 26th Movement

To be explicit (and incidentally to avoid the charge of evading the issues involved), let me offer at this point a formal proposition about the development of the Cuban Revolution. The evolution of the Revolution can best and most accurately be understood as the product of a dynamic inter-relationship between three primary factors. Two of these basic elements, furthermore, are themselves to be understood only in terms of their own self-contained interaction.

One of these major factors is defined by the interaction between Castro's commitment to the Constitution of 1940 (which throughout this essay should be taken to include his commitment to a thoroughgoing social revolution) and the United States. A second is defined by the similar and concurrent interaction between Castro's commitment to the Constitution of 1940 and the other elements that formed the anti-Batista coalition in July, 1958. The third major element is the on-going economic crisis that had started in the last year (or 18 months) of Batista's rule, and for the origins of which Castro bears absolutely no responsibility. When Castro came to power, for example, there were some 700,000 unemployed. The depression was caused by the long-term and worldwide decline in commodity prices that affected all underdeveloped countries, Cuba's drastically unbalanced economy, and Batista's corruption, waste, inefficiency, and mismanagement.

Even at first glance, the complex and compound interaction between all of these variables looks like it is complicated— and it is complicated. All historical reality is complicated, and revolutions are particularly so. But it will not do to deal with the difficulty by falling back upon a simplification based either upon Castro's alleged betrayal, the machinations of the Cuban Communists, or American policy. The picture can only be clarified through a step-by-step analysis of each part of the inter-relationships.

The first advance can be made by getting straight on the nature and the outlook of Castro and his immediate followers who made up the July 26th Movement. Strictly speaking, the July 26th Movement includes only those men and women who began with, or joined, Castro and stayed with him as a very highly integrated force prior to the time, July 20, 1958, when he signed the coalition agreement with other Cuban opposition groups. Hence the analysis must start with them.

Draper's basic argument is that these men and women were middle class. His reason for saying this is that they were middle class in *origin*. Draper sticks to this criteria of *origin* throughout his discussion, even though he makes remarks and offers evidence which implicitly undercut its value and usefulness. Since he introduces Marx to buttress his own argument about the myth of a peasant revolution, it seems appropriate to reintroduce Marx to indicate the very serious weaknesses in Draper's thesis about the middle-class nature of the original July 26th Movement.

Draper calls upon Marx in making the following assertion about the role of the peasants: "For Marx, the notion that the peasants would have been the driving force of a socialist revolution would have been simply unthinkable." The appropriate comment on that proposition has recently been made by George Lichtheim in his fine essay, *Marxism: An Historical and Critical Study*: "Marx himself had cautiously admitted the possibility of a socialist development in Russia (the popular notion to the contrary is based on ignorance)." The main point, however, is not that Draper missed Marx's thinking about the radical force inherent in Russian peasant culture. It is rather that a more general familiarity with Marx might have helped

44

Draper resolve his troubles with the middle-class origins of Castro and his intimate associates.

He might, for example, have exploited his very revealing remark about the "declassed sons and daughters of the middle class." Or his even earlier insight that out of Castro's experience with the peasants in the mountains of Oriente Province, through a process "partly practical and partly emotional, came a determination to revolutionize Cuban society by raising the lowest and most neglected sector to a civilized level of well-being and human dignity."

What is at issue here is the way that Draper keeps talking about Castro and his close associates as middle-class men and women even though he offers various facts and interpretative remarks that make their middle-class origins less and less important in understanding them. Marx wrote reams about avoiding this crucial mistake in analysis. His point was that the concept of class, in order to be useful in a dynamic as opposed to a static analysis and interpretation of events, had to be defined on the basis of actionable categories. Thus the statistics of income distribution do not provide a valid basis for defining class. Neither do social strata defined in terms of the division of labor. Marx insisted that class was defined by reference to two other criteria: (1) the ownership and control of productive property, and (2) a consciousness of class on the part of the human beings involved.

Though his orthodox Communist followers have very seldom emulated his next step, Marx went on to point out that men and women who belonged in one class according to their position in the pattern of property relations could—and did— become members of another class through their conscious identification and action with that second class. For that matter, Marx in his own analysis of capitalism never really developed oɪ used this insight concerning the way in which ideas influenced the economic part of reality. He did exploit the perception to a greater extent in his early writings, in some of his letters and newspaper articles, and in his historical essays interpreting the French and German Revolutions of 1848. His major opus would have been considerably less brittle and schematic if he had sustained that more inclusive approach. He might also in that way have avoided some of his mistakes.

His insights remain valid, however, and can be used with considerable effectiveness in clarifying the evolution of Castro and the original July 26th Movement. This analysis can fairly begin with Draper's reference to the "declassed sons and daughters of the middle class," and his description of their reaction to being confronted with peasant reality. The process of being declassed can occur in one of two ways, or in a combination of both. It can take place as the result of changes in the structure of property relations, and as the result of a personalized experience in being exposed—directly or vicariously—to a different milieu.

In this connection, it is essential to understand that all the contemporary emphasis on the differences between advanced and backward societies has served to obscure at least one very striking similarity. One of the things that occur in very advanced societies, and in underdeveloped countries that have begun to move out of that condition, is a process of declassing which affects children of the established upper- and middle-class families. The reasons behind this experience are quite different in the two cases, but the phenomenon itself is the same.

In the advanced country, technological advances produce organizational changes that impinge ever more oppressively upon the middle-class businessman, farmer, and professional person. Corporate forms of organization and association become the only effective units of operation. This means that the mature, established middle-class entrepreneur experiences an ever increasing disparity between his ideas of the good society and the real society in which he lives. So do his children, particularly of the generations which live through the early phases of the process. In the first sense of class as defined by Marx, they are declassed because their property is losing its effective power in the political and social arenas, as well as in the economic marketplace.

A great deal has been written to the point that Marx was wrong in expecting and predicting the increasing proletarianization of industrial societies. This criticism is valid if the process is taken to mean the driving down of ever larger numbers of people into the conditions of 19th- or early 20th-century industrial day laborers. Marx was correct, however, if proletarianization is viewed in the light of his first definition of class. In terms of their position in the property system, that is to say, an ever larger number of people have been pushed into a lower class. Their incomes have gone up but their effective leverage in the system has gone down. In every realm, in art as well as in economics, they are acted *on* instead of participating *in*. In this sense, at any rate, they have been forced to make a spectator sport out of the functioning of the social system itself.

Referring still to the advanced countries, this experience generally produces a conservative reaction on the part of the originally middle-class individual. It is, for example, the central dynamic explanation of *poujadism* in France, and the phenomena of McCarthyism and later extreme right-wing movements in the United States. Such people and movements cannot really be understood in terms of psychological or psychiatric categories. They are not truly irrational in the sense meant by those disciplines.

Indeed, they are quite lucid in their analysis of what is happening; many of them, for example, talk straight to the point about the underlying changes in the property system. Furthermore, they are not, as their critics often argue, so wholly wide of the mark in attacking the government instead of the corporation. For the idea and the practice of having the state accumulate capital for the corporation has played a very significant role in the corporation's rise to power.

But to call such people radical is to confuse the entire

process and the issues it raises. The program of such protesting middle-class people is reactionary. They retain the ideas and general outlook of the middle class as of the time when that class did enjoy a position in the property system that gave them power and influence. They are far more concerned, incidentally, with recovering their former ability to act upon their environment than they are worried about their status. To this important degree, they understand their own situation better than the academics who write about a status revolution. But these middle-class discontents want to restore the past, and hence they are reactionary.

There is a portion of the mature middle-class generation involved in the process that, generally because of its education and perceptiveness, comes to understand what has happened and either identifies with the new corporate system or acquiesces in the process. Most of the children caught in the transition, especially after the first generation, follow the former course and move routinely and indifferently into the corporate society. Some become disillusioned or discouraged and have in recent years turned up as the Teddy Boys in England and the Beats in the United States. Another group of the children, somewhat larger, has set off in boy scout fashion after their elders who are hiking into the past. A minority have become radicals; so far, however, they have generally confused radicalism with the reformism of the 1930's.

This description and review of the process of declassing— or proletarianization—as it occurs in a familiar advanced society should provide sufficient background to understand how it affects various groups in an underdeveloped society that is moving toward industrialization. In a society such as Cuba, for example, the sons and daughters of both the new middle class and the old neo-feudal aristocratic upper class are subject to the same kind of pressure and difficulty.

More often than not, of course, the children of the traditional upper class enjoy the opportunity to shift over into the modern system. As with the landed aristocrats of Tudor and Stuart England, for example, their parents generally manage to exchange a high property position in the agrarian-commercial society for a similar place in the new system. This is not always the case, however, and Latin America may in the future produce a growing number of upper-class children who turn up in reform and radical movements. For one thing, they come out of a tradition of social responsibility which produces a feeling of antagonism toward middle-class values.

The children of middle-class families in such societies as Cuba face a far more difficult problem. On the one hand, they are educated and indoctrinated with the values of their successful middle-class parents, *and with the expectation that the future is theirs*. On the other hand, their society is not shifting over to the new system at a rate fast enough to create enough places in the property system to absorb them. That disparity between expectation and reality produces in many of them a severely critical attitude toward the status quo.

This dissatisfaction, coupled with personal considerations, prompts many such children of the middle class to go into politics. Almost all of them initially do so with the values of the middle class. This means that the majority of them become enthusiastic and active reformers in the traditional and honorable sense of that term. Unless they become thoroughly discouraged, or unless their formal and informal education changes their understanding of the situation, that is what most of them remain.

But such education, often coupled with intense personal experiences as students or young men and women, does drive a minority of these declassed children toward the political left. A few jump almost immediately to socialism or communism. Most move first to a bourgeois radicalism. In Latin America, moreover, the inherent romanticism of that position is strongly reinforced by cultural factors of a particularly deep and persuasive kind. The whole concept and symbolism of the male,

49

for example, strengthens the Prometheus-like character of the ideal bourgeois radical. The combination of influences is very apt to produce an image of the political hero as a man who can socialize the society without socializing the economy.

This picture of the dynamic, even explosive, Latin American middle-class child become romantic bourgeois radical provides a good likeness of Castro, and of the majority of the men and women in the original July 26th Movement. The inclination to think of them as Latin American populists is rather strong. There is no first-rate study of Latin American populism, and it may be that the idea would prove less useful after such a careful investigation had been made, but the original July 26th Movement did have many characteristics exhibited by populism in other societies.

To begin with, the majority of populist leaders have traditionally come from non-peasant classes. Here the evidence concerning the July 26th Movement is impressive. Draper's point about their middle-class *origin* is correct. Next, populists have usually organized and operated as loose congeries of independent or semi-independent groups. Castro's early operations, and his slowness in forming a coalition with other anti-Batista groups, are quite striking in this connection.

Another characteristic of such populist movements stems from the enervating experience of coping with powerful governments over an extended period of time. Populists have usually known repeated defeats which instilled in them a sense of humiliation; but which also encouraged the converse attitudes of contempt for the existing government, a particularly acute sensitiveness to criticism, and a propensity to anticipate trouble. Castro's edginess on many (though not all) issues, his attitude toward Batista, and his repeated fears of a counter-revolutionary move by Batista are examples of parallel phenomena.

With respect to their program, populists have never been noted for original or highly integrated ideas. They have generally operated with a rather casual, vague, and certainly non-

Marxian version of the theory that existing society can only be understood as a class struggle between the haves and the have-nots. This was obviously typical of Castro and other members of the July 26th Movement as they came to power. Sartre and Draper are correct in pointing out that the July 26th group lacked any formal theory—or ideology—which served as a basis for its action.

Ernesto ("Che") Guevara was very explicit in making this point about his associates. "The principal actors of this revolution had no coherent theoretical criteria; but it cannot be said that they were ignorant of the various concepts of history, society, economics, and revolution which are being discussed in the world today." Castro and other participants in the Revolution have said much the same kind of thing.

But it is very easy to over-emphasize this lack of an ideology. The tendency to do this, which is evident in every account of the Revolution, probably stems from the mid-20th century propensity to think of all revolutions in terms of the Bolshevik Revolution of 1917. Compared with the Russians and their Marxist doctrine as it existed in 1917 (and even more, to the oversimplified and schematic version of it that most commentators work with), the Cubans may indeed seem at first glance to be almost anti-intellectual. But the leaders of the July 26th Movement were not *really* running about without *any* ideas on their minds. It is accurate to say that they lacked a tightly-knit, neatly tailored set of intellectual threads. But it is very misleading to go beyond that and say that they were bereft of any inter-related ideas.

It is relevant to recall, in this connection, that the rough and ready populist kind of have *vs* have-not interpretation of society inclined many Russian populists toward Marxism long before the Bolshevik Revolution occurred; and the same attitude also prompted many American populists on the prairie to support the socialism of Eugene Debs. And, as will be seen, the Cuban Constitution of 1940 could very easily provide men

51

who took it seriously with an integrated set of ideas that has many of the characteristics of an ideology. It is most certainly an ideological document, and much of what the leaders of the Cuban Revolution have done can be seen as a manifestation of the outlook it symbolizes.

Populists have also viewed the peasants as martyrs, and Castro's speeches stating and elaborating that theme must have become somewhat tiring even to the Cuban peasants themselves. His less generous attitude toward urban labor is also indicative of this attitude. As for their objectives, populists have traditionally stressed two goals—social justice and social equality. They have never been indifferent to formal, institutionalized representative government; nor have they relegated it to a low place in their hierarchy of values. But they have generally tended to give more emphasis to the job of changing society.

The populist argument on this point is that representative government can only function in an honest and equitable manner after the basic changes in the system have been made. Castro and his first government in Cuba were actually very candid and straightforward in announcing and explaining their decision to delay elections, and their argument ran along these lines. Castro's later remark that "real democracy is not possible for hungry people" is a classic statement of the populist axiom concerning the relationship between politics and economics.

Whatever the value of this comparison and analogy between populism and Castro's original July 26th Movement as a description, analysis, and explanation of that group, it would seem to clarify one crucial point. Draper's operating description of those men and women as middle-class citizens is wrong. They were not middle-class in the fundamental sense that they acted as middle-class leaders either before or after they came to power. Contrary to what Draper says, they did not follow "a middle class way-of-life." It is true, as Castro and others have often observed, that they were "still full of petty bourgeois prejudices." But they did not think of themselves as typical middle-class citizens, and their minds did not function in that classic pattern.

The final validity of this estimate is underscored by two events: Castro's politics in the first week after Batista fled the island, and the commitment of Castro and the original July 26th Movement to the Constitution of 1940. His politics were strictly Jacobin, and the Constitution of 1940 is anything but a middle-class document.

Batista abandoned Cuba before his army wholly disintegrated. Some remnants were taken over by vigorously anti-Castro officers, like Major General Eulogio Cantillo Porras, who attempted to block a complete victory by Castro and the July 26th Movement. Other elements in the general coalition formed to fight Batista on July 20, 1958, which is so misleadingly confused with the original July 26th Movement by most commentators, also desired to limit Castro's power. In one sense, at any rate, the most revealing opposition came from several small student militia units within the Directorio Revolucionario 13 de Marzo.

Those students were certainly middle-class in Draper's use of the term, and they sensed—perhaps even understood very clearly—Castro's Jacobin outlook. They were in any event close to the mark. Castro responded to all such opposition by calling a general strike to enforce the across-the-board acceptance of his leadership. His victory is of course significant, but here the crucial point is that such behavior is hardly the response that one associates with middle-class leadership.

5

The Cuban Constitution of 1940

Having considered the underlying outlook of Castro and the original July 26th Movement, we must next examine another of the basic factors involved in the evolution of the Revolution—the Cuban Constitution of 1940. One of the most tantalizing features of all the American writing on the Revolution is the way all the authors shy away from any straightforward review of the document. They talk of it and around it but never about it.

But one remark by Draper, even though he never follows through on it, raises enough of this curtain of silence for the reader to ask some very pointed and fundamental questions about his entire interpretation of the Revolution. "Castro promised," he charges, "to restore Cuban democracy and make it work, not a 'direct' or 'people's' democracy but the one associated with the 1940 Constitution, which was so radical that much of it, especially the provision for agrarian reform, was never implemented."

Now that phrase, *which was so radical,* fairly thunders into the mind of the reader. The question comes so fast that it seems to be a natural reflex. What could be *that* radical about a constitution written and adopted in a country dominated by conservative elements dependent upon the support of Batista and the United States?

The only way to find out is to review the history of the Constitution and then examine the document itself. It may be useful at the outset, in view of the way Draper and other commentators bypass this crucial part of the story, to note that a full and excellent English translation is available in Robert H. Fitzgibbon's collection of *The Constitutions of the Americas.* One gains considerable insight into the Revolution by reading

55

the Constitution and then, with that background, giving careful consideration to Castro's famous "History Will Absolve Me" speech, which is built around many explicit references to the spirit and to the specific provisions of the Constitution.

In the broadest sense, the Cuban Constitution of 1940 was the product of the failure of American policy between 1898 and 1936. It represented, and was the creation of, a basic consensus among conservatives, liberals, and radicals who, in the context of a deep depression, defined Cuba's future within a nationalistic, anti-American framework, and in terms of an integrated, socially responsible society and government concerned with economic diversification and development.

Cuban conservatives who were largely dependent upon American business operations, and who opposed a serious reform and social welfare program, fought the Constitution even as it was proposed and drafted. Those men could not prevent its adoption, but they were able—until the advent of Castro— to keep the Constitution from being used as a guide to, and as an active instrument of, government action. They accomplished this through their political and economic power in the island (including their connections with American leaders), by taking advantage of the war and postwar boom which did serve for many years to keep social discontent just below the revolutionary level, and by smearing any effort to implement the Constitution as a threat to Cuban freedom, liberty, and the tradition of Latin *joie de vivre*.

During the 1930's, however, such conservatives operated under much less favorable circumstances, and they were temporarily defeated by a coalition of aroused and angry Cubans. In many respects, therefore, the Cuban Constitution was a product of the short-run—as well as the long-term—failure of American policy. New Deal intervention did manage to topple Grau's government, but that very success only exacerbated an unstable political and economic situation. No single party or coalition could establish and maintain enough routine authority to proceed with the work of governing and improving Cuba.

After Grau was defeated, it is true that American economic policy, in the form of the sugar quota and a reciprocity treaty, was slightly less harmful and did promote some recovery through a modest revival of the sugar industry. But the improvement was constantly threatened by the general depression, and by persistent American pressure on Cuba to repay its debts of $80 million to private American entrepreneurs and to commit its economy to the traditional imperial pattern of selling some sugar to the United States and buying great quantities of American manufactured goods. Cuba was a disorganized society on the edge of stagnation and chaos.[1] As a result, and though they were weakened by dissension and factionalism, the critics of the status quo enjoyed a basic advantage over the conservatives who would have been content to go along with the existing order and wait for the tie with the United States to produce slow, uneven improvement.

Given this situation, it may not seem too surprising, after a moment's reflection, to realize that the movement toward the Constitution began when Batista used the army to break the general strike of 1935. His action symbolized a decision to take charge of the country in an overt, positive manner and establish the necessary minimum of order and stability. Once he began to move, Batista's bid for leadership had important consequences. His candidate, Miguel Mariano Gomez, won the subsequent election in 1936, the Cuban Congress began to function regularly for the first time since 1933, and Grau shortly (in July, 1936) went into exile. As Grau left, Gomez announced that "something must be done" to remedy the appalling conditions. Reforms were needed, but Gomez emphasized the deeper aspects of the crisis. Cuba had been governed for five years through a hodge-podge of executive decrees and incidental

---

1. A concise review of the situation is provided by Russell B. Porter in a series of articles in the *New York Times* of July 4, 5, 7, and 9, 1936.

legislation that was disjoined and insufficient to the problems at hand. Gomez and Batista therefore called for a constitutional convention to establish "a semi-parliamentary form of government, with a premier and cabinet."

Radicals and other critics had been agitating for fundamental changes ever since 1929, and in part Gomez was simply moving to blunt their strength and appeal while simultaneously consolidating his own (and Batista's) position in the country. But neither this truth, nor the ultimate nature of the Batista regime, should be allowed to confuse one's understanding of the situation as it existed in 1936. The central feature of that period involves Batista's basic and sincere desire to create a corporate state within the Catholic and Latin traditions of that kind of society and government; an integrated, organic state that would improve the lot of the poor as part of a general program of economic growth.

One related point is equally clear: that, having consolidated his own power in the army, and the army's position as the court of last resort in Cuban politics, Batista was willing, between 1935 and the presidential election of 1940, to work within the system of representative government in his efforts to create such a corporate state. Batista later increasingly relied on the use of force—intimidation, torture, and terrorism— to maintain his own power. Finally, of course, his regime became a nightmare of horror, corruption, and failure.

But the Constitution of 1940 cannot be explained or understood unless one realizes that Batista and his era evolved through several periods. The Batista of the years 1935-1940 was a man who wanted to legitimatize his power through the establishment of a corporate state, whose concern for a better Cuba was real and not sham, and whose basic political strategy involved striking an alliance with reformers and radicals (including Communists) in Cuba while bargaining for more aid from the United States. The point is not that Batista was a "good guy" who became a "bad guy," or a liberal who became a conservative, or even a demagogue of the Huey Long variety. American stereotypes are irrelevant and misleading. Batista was a socially conscious conservative in the Catholic and Latin tradition who was also driven by inordinate ambition. His ambition ultimately destroyed his commitment to the kind of socially responsible corporate state that initially served as his ideal and as his model for Cuba.

"I believe Cuba should have a renovated democracy," Batista explained candidly in July, 1936, "under which there should be discipline of the masses and of institutions so that we can establish a progressive state under which the masses may be taught a new idea of democracy and learn to discipline themselves. . . . We want to teach the masses that capital and labor both are necessary and should cooperate. We want to drive out utopian ideas."[1]

Batista operated on two levels throughout 1936 and 1937. The movement for a Constitutional Constituent Assembly, which he encouraged, was organized with support from labor unions, farmers, conservative but moderate business elements, and the reform and radical political parties. On his own, meanwhile, Batista began to build a personal following and attempted to infiltrate and lead the groundswell for a new constitution. Beginning in the fall of 1936, for example, he used the army to build and staff new schools in the interior of Cuba. He even advocated a special tax on raw sugar (of 9 cents a bag) to finance the program.

Then, on July 25, 1937, he came forward with a dramatic Three Year Plan designed to pull Cuba out of the depression, improve the conditions of the poor, and generate sustained prosperity. Based on the principle of a government-directed economy, the plan included tight controls over the sugar, tobacco, and mining industries, a new currency system including a

---

1. Batista: remarks during an interview reported in the *New York Times,* July 5, 1936. Both the tone and the language of this interview reveal the inherent corporatism of Batista's thought.

national bank, reforestation and water-development projects, distribution of some land to the poor, control of the labor market for Cuban nationals, government intervention to settle disputes between capital and labor, and various health and educational programs.

Batista's proposal was immediately criticized by reformers who claimed he had merely appropriated every idea they had offered since 1895—he was ridiculed as the author of a "300 Year Plan"—attacked by radicals who called his program "a form of tropical fascism," and opposed by businessmen who thought he was carrying responsible conservatism a good deal too far. But he also won considerable support among the poor if only because his was the only concrete plan being offered in the crisis. One group of 2,000 demonstrators who gathered to "demand that large land holdings in Cuba be divided up," used the chant of "Viva Batista!" as their rallying cry. Batista encouraged such agitation and tried to turn it into solid support for himself by actually distributing some land in the Pinar del Rio Province.

Whatever its future might have been under different circumstances, the Three Year Plan was defeated by the depressed economic conditions it was supposed to counteract. The country, as one American observer reported, was "suffering from an attack of the jitters" brought on by the uncertainty of sugar prices and the policy of the United States. Throughout the period, for example, demonstrators repeatedly avowed their support for Mexico in its dispute with America over the nationalization of Mexican oil resources, and called for "the total economic liberty" of Cuba from American control.

But the power of the United States could not be done away with through demonstrations and slogans. President Gomez was not exaggerating when he told Secretary Hull that "he could not bear to contemplate the plight of the Cuban people if the economic benefits received from the United States were taken away from them"—as Hull implied might be done if

Cuba did not pay its obligations to American business firms. The Cuban tragedy is defined in that one remark: the benefits were pitifully small, but they did make a crucial difference in the mid-1930's.

Batista's trip to Washington in November, 1938, was brought about by this general crisis. Washington was seeking to use him to preserve its control over the island, and Batista was playing the very risky game of trying to reassure and satisfy American leaders while seeking to build a reform coalition at home. He succeeded in the sense that he won the backing of Hull, Welles, and Roosevelt, but he failed in the more important sense that the price of his short-run victory was a set of long-term conditions that made it impossible for him to erect his corporate state.[1]

After he returned to Cuba, Batista supervised the election of delegates to the Constitutional Constituent Assembly. He played it straight. Grau was allowed to return from exile in time to campaign effectively, and the election itself was one of the most honest in the political history of the island. The results gave Grau and other critics of the government a slight majority in the assembly. But a broad consensus among the delegates soon became apparent, and the Constitution of 1940 was the joint product of the corporate philosophy of the Batista bloc and the reform and radical ideas of Grau and other opposition groups. Both blocs supported extensive social welfare provisions, agreed that the government should exercise a commanding position in the economy, and shared an intense nationalism dedicated to making Cuba vastly more independent of American influence and control.

These characteristics become apparent in the first article

---

1. Various stories (one told by Batista) claim that Roosevelt made suggestions to Batista about the proposed constitution. These tales jibe with Roosevelt's known propensity to play at such long-distance reform, and probably have some substance. But the Cuban Constitution of 1940 cannot be understood in such terms.

of the Constitution. "Cuba is an independent and sovereign State organized as a unitary and democratic republic for the enjoyment of political freedom, social justice, individual and collective welfare, and human solidarity."

The nationalism is obvious. But so, too, is the tension inherent in either a conservative (corporate) or a radical (socialist) effort to resolve the conflicts between individualism and social justice, between the individual and the general welfare, and between the individual and the social group. Draper's quite casual implication that returning to the Constitution of 1940 involves a relatively simple act loses much of its persuasiveness immediately one begins to read the document.

This reaction is further strengthened when one comes upon the general provisions holding that the overriding rule for interpreting the Constitution is the principle of social justice—not the written articles or laws based thereon. For all intents and purposes, one careful reading of the nearly 300 articles of the Constitution suggests that Draper's central arraignment of Castro for betraying the Revolution is a very forced, not to say irrelevant, proposition. It is simply not the proper question to ask in order to follow the development of the Cuban Revolution.

The basic political right established in the Constitution is "to vote, according to the provisions of the law, in the elections and referendums that may be held in the Republic." A later article adds that the people "express their opinions upon the questions submitted to them by means of the referendum." "The organization of political parties and associations is free. However, no political groupings of race, sex, or class may be formed." Finally, all political rights "may be suspended in all or in part of the national territory, for a period not greater than forty-five calendar days, whenever the security of the State may require it."

Several features of these provisions call for further comment. The Constitution refers to elections or referendums that "may be held." It does not establish a set schedule of elections, and would appear to envisage a parliamentary system in which the government periodically goes to the voters on substantive issues rather than an elective process based on chronologically defined tenure. In this connection, moreover, a revolutionary government would be wholly within its constitutional powers to set the first election at its pleasure.

The authorization to suspend political rights for considerations of "the security of the State" is clear and definite. A revolutionary government, furthermore, would not initially be bound by the constitutional requirement involving approval by the legislature when such action is first taken by the executive. There would be no revolutionary legislature until elections were held. It is also clear that the stated time limit of 45 days can easily be extended through the device of interrupting the ban for 24 hours once every six weeks.

This kind of constitutional warrant for suspending political rights raises several crucial issues, and can be severely criticized. A similar article in the constitution of the Weimar Republic, for example, offered an opening that Hitler used very effectively once he had been voted into power. On the other hand, and as the German instance suggests, the provision exists in a good many constitutions written and adopted after World War I, and the Cuban version is neither new nor unique. In any event, it is in the Constitution, and Castro can not be held responsible for that.

Finally, it should not be imagined that such executive power is unique to the kind of system established by the Constitution in Cuba. The office of the President of the United States enjoys many powers that various presidents have exploited to the hilt. Many of those actions were taken unilaterally and were sanctioned by the Congress only after the fact—and even then only under emergency conditions involving war or the threat of war. This should be kept in mind, because Castro invoked the identical reason in mid-1959 for an indefinite postponement of elections.

It seems necessary to be explicit about such matters because of the very human propensity to criticize what an executive does with such power in terms of his alleged usurpation of authority. This badly confuses the issues. The first point is always the one involving the existence of the power, and it is clear that the legal grant of authority exists in the Cuban Constitution of 1940.

For all these reasons, it would seem apparent that the Cuban Constitution of 1940 does not emphasize political rights by way of establishing a system in which American-style politics is the first thing to be guaranteed and the last thing to be circumscribed. The two principal reasons for this are not very difficult to uncover. One involves the long and entrenched Latin American tradition and practice of rule by an elite of one kind or another. This is such an inherent part of the culture, and is so well-established by all studies of the region, that there is no need to belabor the point.

The other explanation is implicit in the Constitution of 1940. It defines the state as the agent of, and charges it with the responsibilty for, economic development, social welfare and justice, and the recovery and protection of Cuban national sovereignty. Consider, for example, the following explicit statements of these responsibilities:

Article 3: "The Republic shall not conclude or ratify pacts or treaties that in any form limit or menace national sovereignty or the integrity of the territory."

Article 60: "The State shall employ all the resources in its power to provide an occupation for everyone."

Article 88: "The subsoil belongs to the State. . . . Land, forests, and concessions for the exploitation of the subsoil, utilization of waters, means of transportation, and every other enterprise of public service, must be exploited in a manner favorable to the social welfare."

Article 90: "The law shall stipulate the maximum amount of property that each person or corporation may possess for each type of exploitation. . . . The law shall restrictively limit acquisition and possession of land by foreign persons and companies, and shall adopt measures tending to revert the land to Cuban ownership."

Article 271: "The State shall direct the course of the national economy for the benefit of the people in order to assure a proper existence for each individual. . . . It shall be a primary duty of the State to promote national agriculture and industry, facilitating their diversification as sources of public wealth and collective benefit."

Article 264: "The State shall, without impairing the other means within its range, regulate the development of the national wealth by means of the execution of public works payable entirely or in part by those directly benefited."

Article 272: "Ownership and possession of real property and the exploitation of agricultural, industrial, commercial, banking, and any other kind of enterprise or business by foreigners . . . are subject in an obligatory manner to the same conditions as the law may establish for nationals, which must in all cases be adjusted to the socio-economic interests of the nation."

Article 275: "The law shall regulate by administration the planting and milling of sugar cane, and may reduce these operations to the minimum limit imposed by the socio-economic necessity of maintaining the sugar industry on the basis of the division of the two great factors participating in its development: the manufacturers or producers of the sugar, and the farmers or tenants producing the cane."

Article 280: "Money and banking are submitted to the regulation and control of the State. . . . The State may require that its capital be subscribed by the banks already existing."

These provisions are of themselves so broad and far-reaching in their implications that comment seems largely unnecessary. The Constitution of 1940 recognized "the existence and legitimacy of private property" (Article 87), but the authorization of expropriation "for a cause justified by public utility or social interests" (Article 24) clearly gives the State the power to implement its other, primary, responsibilities.

Similar circumstances surround the "right of organization . . . for employers, private employees, and workers." In the same Article 69, for example, the right is precisely defined as holding "for the exclusive purposes of their economic-social activity." Article 84 tightens that specification by requiring that "problems arising from the relations between capital and labor shall be submitted to committees of conciliation."

To return to the obligations and responsibilities of the State, the Constitution charges it (Article 79) to "support the creation of low-cost dwellings for workers;" and, in Title IV, Section 2, with the establishment of a general educational system. And finally, "in order to assure compliance with social legislation, the State shall provide for the supervision and inspection of enterprises" (Article 85).

The character and extent of such social legislation is rather fully defined by the Constitution itself. Article 65 specifies that "social insurance benefits are established as irrenounceable and imprescriptible rights of workers." Compensation for industrial accidents is mandatory: pensions and survivor benefits for employees of the national, provincial, and municipal governments "are to be based on the needs of the recipients." Minimum wages are likewise mandatory, so also an eight-hour day, a 44-hour week, and paid vacations of one month. And, as might have been expected, the wages, hours, and conditions of employment for women and children are spelled out in considerable detail.

There was very little comment in the United States about this notably radical constitution, either as it was being written or when it went into operation on October 10, 1940. In its volume of published documents covering that year, for example, the State Department does not print a single reference to any discussion of the document among American policy-makers, or between them and the Cubans. The section on Cuba is taken up with economic questions at issue between the two countries. It is true, of course, that the Department of State chooses not to print many important—even vital—documents, but there is no public record of any discussion of the subject. And one can hardly imagine Hull restraining himself if he considered the issue of any great importance. He did not even mention it in his *Memoirs*.

The Department of Labor did print a short summary of the labor and social welfare provisions in the October, 1940, issue of the *Monthly Labor Review*. But even that was prepared by a correspondent in Havana. *Business Week* of October 12, 1940, was the only general American magazine to offer any pointed comment.[1] Given the magazine's audience, and its conception of its role and responsibility, this is perfectly understandable. American business leaders could be expected to show considerable interest in a constitution which gave the national government such broad powers over the economy of the island.

The magazine's remarks, moreover, were very perceptive. It made two points that are essential to any understanding of events since January 1, 1959. A 20-year depth of vision in such matters is unusual, and should be noted and praised. "Sudden and drastic enforcement of the new regulations," the editors remarked, "is not anticipated. Cuba is too closely tied to the United States, both economically and politically." It would have been difficult to put the truth any more neatly. *The Cuban Constitution of 1940 could not be put into operation without disrupting the basic substance and tone of traditional American-Cuban relations.* The editors of *Business Week* also understood the implicit meaning of the document for Cuban society. "Whether or not it is ever enforced," they noted, almost in warning, "Cuba's spectacular new charter has created a power-

---

1. The *New York Times* carried a good many stories about the Constitutional Assembly, but no thorough evaluation.

ful implement for social and economic reforms." They were correct, and that aspect of the Constitution is precisely what upset Cuban conservatives who opposed such reform. "Capital, commerce, and industry strongly opposed approval of various clauses of the Constitution," noted a reporter of the *New York Times* on September 29, 1940, "and it is freely predicted that modifications will be necessary within the near future." The modifications took the form of simply ignoring the basic spirit, and many explicit provisions, of the Constitution.

These comments in *Business Week* and the *New York Times* serve to define the central point about the Cuban Revolution of 1959. *The Constitution of 1940 could not be put into operation save through a profound social revolution.* And anyone who undertook to breathe life into the Cuban Constitution of 1940, particularly in the context of an existing economic depression, would immediately find himself confronted by many difficulties and many opponents. That is precisely what happened to Fidel Castro.

6

Castro and the Challenge Inherent in the Constitution of 1940

The grave charge that Castro betrayed the Cuban Revolution seems at first hearing to be a direct and uncomplicated accusation. But even a moment's reflection serves to raise a troublesome point. Even if the interpretation is valid, it does not tell us much about the evolution of the Revolution per se unless we are told *why* Castro turned Judas.

The only straightforward answer to that question is the one provided by those, like Nathaniel Weyl,[1] who assert—but have yet to prove—that Castro was a Communist from the beginning of the story. Other commentators have hinted or implied, with varying degrees of sophistication, that the key lies in Castro's drive for power. But this single-factor interpretation has pretty much had its day in sociology, as well as in history, and few still consider it satisfactory as an explanation of complex human affairs.

To say that a man in politics wants power is to speak the truth, but it is to do so at such a level of generality—even banality—as to mouth one of those dangerous whole truths which distort reality as much as, or even more than, the more notorious half-truths.

It is more fruitful to review the natural history of the accusation. The first use of it that I have been able to find came in a remark attributed to a middle- or upper-class Cuban printed in a news story in the *New York Times* during April, 1959. It appeared again in that form, but was more often used by the reporters themselves. Even so, the indictment was not

---

1. Nathaniel Weyl, *Red Star Over Cuba* (New York, Devin-Adair, 1960).

repeated very often in the early days of the Revolution, and did not become a cliché until later.

Draper revived, amplified, and developed the brief for betrayal in his well-known series of articles in *The New Leader* and *Encounter*. Other commentators who were critical of the Revolution quickly borrowed the thesis and used it broadcast. Finally, the United States made it the central theme of its White Paper of April 3, 1961.

This course of events suggests rather strongly that the charge of betrayal originated with Cubans who had become disenchanted with Castro's revolutionary program, and who were either on the verge of, or had actually committed themselves to, opposition in varying degrees and forms to his government.

The question thus arises as to which charge of betrayal should be considered in any evaluation. Let us dismiss at the outset, on the grounds that they are clearly derivative, all but those presented by the Cubans who talked with American reporters in the spring of 1959, and the one developed by Draper.

The Cubans whose remarks are recorded criticized Castro's early economic measures because they claimed to be hurt by them, and opposed his outcries against the United States on the grounds that Cuba's economy—and their personal prosperity—was wholly dependent upon the American sugar market. This antagonism toward Castro is logical and understandable. Nor is there any reason not to sympathize with the difficulties of such people. But their attacks do not involve any betrayal by Castro. The critics were frightened and angry, and used the word in a personal and emotional way.

Let us therefore turn to Draper. His argument involves four main acts of betrayal involving the promise of elections, the promise to return to the Constitution of 1940, the nature and extent of agrarian reform, and the bringing of Communists into the Cuban government.

One general consideration must be kept clearly in mind throughout the ensuing discussion. Draper implicitly discounts, and almost literally ignores, the fact that a fundamental social revolution—thwarted and delayed since 1933—was set in motion by the triumph of Castro. He writes about Castro's betrayal of the Revolution almost as though the Revolution itself was a schoolbook exercise in politics.

Draper's world of revolution is cut of cardboard. There are no troubled and perplexed men. No human beings struggling with conflicting ideas, ideals, or loyalties. And no people changing their minds as the result of thought, or of exposure to new ideas and experiences. None of that troublesome reality for Draper. Just men of bad faith betraying a noble revolution.

Draper explicitly discounts the entire complex of circumstances and momentum that are inherent in such an upheaval. "Fidel Castro and his inner circle have never been innocent victims of circumstances." The use of the word *"innocent"* is terribly misleading: no leaders of any revolution could be innocent in the sense he implies in his employment of the term. Of course Castro and his close associates in the July 26th Movement wanted a social revolution. They had been hard at it for most of a decade.

Draper's formulation confuses the entire issue of men being caught up in circumstances which confronted them with extremely hard choices involving not only the basic question of abandoning the Revolution, but hundreds of lesser ones concerning the how and the when of trying to put their program into operation. Draper declines to admit into his analysis the three most crucial elements of the entire situation. First, Castro and the original July 26th Movement were out to make a fundamental social revolution in Cuba—to transform the society into something different and better. Second, a commitment to the Cuban Constitution of 1940 not only justified, but demanded such a revolution. And finally, any effort to make such a revolution would provoke opposition within Castro's coalition of June, 1958, and with the United States.

The key to Draper's entire analysis and interpretation of

Castro's Revolution appears in one sentence. "Since Castro took power without a real ideology, a real army, or a real party, he could conceivably have survived without them only by making his power consistent with his promises, and thus holding his original backing together. . . . This is precisely what he chose not to do." But as Draper seems not to understand, the facts do not fit such a neat pattern.

It is much closer to the truth to say that Castro had an implicit ideology in his commitments to fundamental change and to the Constitution of 1940, and as he acted on those commitments he was continually faced with extremely difficult choices. Either he could abandon or drastically modify his commitments or he could face up to the opposition engendered by those commitments, muster what general and specific support he could, and fight through to effect the changes implicit in his romantic radicalism, his identification with the masses, and the Constitution of 1940.

The crucial point is that a commitment to the Constitution of 1940 could not be honored by giving up on the fundamental social revolution. Neither Draper nor anyone else can have it both ways on this issue. For if the commitment to the Constitution is at the heart of the matter, then Castro was not promising a middle-class revolution. He is not, as Draper claims, a middle-class revolutionary turning the Revolution against the middle class. He is instead a radical revolutionary engendering increasing opposition from the upper and middle classes. Draper and others may not approve of Castro's determination to make a fundamental social revolution, or of the way he tied that objective to the Constitution of 1940, but neither action involves any betrayal on the part of Castro.

This can be demonstrated at the outset through an examination of Castro's position on elections, and his commitment to the Constitution of 1940. He talked consistently between 1953 and 1959 of holding elections at the end of the first year after Batista was deposed. On January 6, 1959, however, the new government announced candidly and publicly that this would not occur for 18 months.

Four features of this action deserve attention. First, it was taken by a government that represented the full revolutionary coalition. It was not effected through a coup by Castro. It took place at the outset of the period of which Berle says that "the aggregate morale of the Cuban Revolution was democratic, anti-dictatorial and anti-Communist." Second, the move was constitutional. Third, it was done publicly. And fourth, the government's explanation was relevant and to the point: elections, to be meaningful, should come after the Batista mess had been cleaned up, and after the basic revolutionary changes had been put into effect. Then the election would serve as a judgment on those performances.

On February 28, 1959, the government extended the period of no elections another six months, making it two years in all. And still later, in April, Castro spoke of an even longer interval. Both announcements were public, both included straightforward explanations tied to the revolutionary program, and both occurred while the Revolution was still in the phase described by Berle.

To call this performance a betrayal is to stretch the word so far beyond its denotation as to change fundamentally its meaning. That is the only way that Draper's indictment on this point can be validated. The postponement of elections does, however, provide an insight into the kind of things that a commitment to the Constitution of 1940 actually involved.

Let us turn, therefore, to Castro's involvement with that document as of the moment he came to power at the head of the revolutionary coalition. In his justly famous speech before the Batista court trying him for rebellion in 1953, which takes its title—"History Will Absolve Me"—from his parting cry of defiance, Castro had this to say about what he would have done if he had succeeded: "The first revolutionary law would have restored sovereignty to the people and proclaimed the

73

Constitution of 1940 as the true supreme law of the state, until such time as the people should decide to modify it or to change it." The commitment is clear enough, and he repeated it in 1957 and 1958.

Given the radical nature of the Constitution—and even Draper admits that—the basic issue would seem to be settled. But Castro went on in his 1953 speech to say things which clarify his own conception of that commitment. Most important of all, he tied the overthrow of Batista and the reassertion of the Constitution of 1940 to "profound changes in the social system." The revolutionary government fully intended to claim the power to make such alterations in the status quo and to use it. "The revolutionary movement, as the momentous incarnation of this sovereignty, the only source of legitimate power, would have assumed all the faculties inherent to it, except that of modifying the Constitution itself: In other words it would have assumed the legislative, executive and judicial powers."

Castro's definition of the people that he gave in behalf of himself and his original followers further emphasized this determination to use a triumph over Batista to carry through a social revolution. "When we speak of the people," he explained, "we do not mean the comfortable ones, the conservative elements of the nation. . . . The *people* means the vast unredeemed masses." That remark should incidentally establish once and for all the non-middle class nature of Castro's outlook, and that of his close associates. It is even more important, however, in indicating the inherent radicalism of Castro's thought.

He provided many examples in 1953 of the way that radicalism was interwoven with his commitment to the Constitution of 1940. As, for example, when he spoke of "two essential articles of our Constitution. One of these," he explained, "orders the outlawing of feudal estates by indicating the maximum area of land any person or entity can possess for each type of agricultural enterprise, by adopting measures which would tend to revert the land to the Cubans." Then he turned to the Constitutional proviso that charges the State with primary responsibility for economic development. This article, Castro remarked in 1953, "categorically orders the State to use all means at its disposal to provide employment to all those who lack it and to insure a decent livelihood to each manual laborer or intellectual."

Given this proof that Castro understood the radical nature of the Constitution of 1940, and that he intended to use the power inherent in a revolutionary victory within that framework, his outline of the crucial issues facing a successful revolution becomes particularly relevant. "The problems concerning land, the problem of industrialization, the problem of housing, the problem of unemployment, the problem of education, and the problem of the health of the people; these are the six problems we would take immediate steps to resolve, along with the restoration of public liberties and political democracy."

Now the structure and phrasing of that sentence very strongly suggest that Castro understood, certainly implicitly and perhaps explicitly, that the process of meeting Cuba's fundamental needs might, in practice, conflict with the immediate restoration of formal and full political freedom. This bears directly on Castro's pledge to return to the Constitution because that same potential conflict—and a similar one concerning the role of the state in economic matters—is inherent in the document itself.

Finally, Castro went on in his remarks of 1953 to emphasize two of those reforms. His movement would "proceed immediately to industrialize the country." And again: "the need to industrialize the country is urgent." In all such references, Castro stressed the active role of the state. Sometimes he did so by mocking the lethargy of the Batista government. Other times he did so directly. That stress not only validates his understanding of the need for government initiative and control in the process of rapid industrialization, but it documents his understanding of the Constitution's authorization for, and even directive to undertake, that kind of diversification.

Castro approached the agricultural problem with rather more emphasis on overall direction and coordination than Draper is willing to acknowledge. Draper wants to decide this issue, which is a significant one over and beyond his indictment of Castro, on the basis of his translation of the speech as against an official Cuban translation.

The official version reads: "We . . . would promote agricultural cooperatives with a single technical, professional direction in farming and cattle raising. Finally, we would provide resources, equipment, protection, and useful guidance to the peasants."

Draper's personal, literal translation from a Cuban edition has Castro speak of "encouraging agricultural cooperatives for the common use of costly equipment, cold storage, and a uniform professional direction in cultivation and breeding, and, finally, to facilitate assistance, equipment, protection, and useful knowledge to the farming population." He then says, on the basis of the difference, that cooperatives "obviously occupied a minor place in the general scheme; they were intended, in the traditional meaning of cooperatives, to service independent landowners."

From a reading of both versions, it is clear that Draper is correct about the omission of the phrase concerning "costly equipment" from the official English version. It is also true, at least in my opinion, that Draper's literal translation does some violence to the feel of the original. A literal translation is not necessarily an accurate translation. But arguments over translations, particularly when the real issues lie elsewhere, are notoriously unproductive.

The problem can more nearly be resolved by reference to other considerations. Point one is that both Draper and the official version agree on the key word *"direction"* in the sentence specifying the role of the cooperatives and their relationship to the farmer. This is not meant as a general educational service, as in the American system of county agricultural agents, because that function and responsibility is referred to in a separate passage. It is meant as direction, to use Draper's phrase, "in cultivation and breeding."

Now given the provisions of the Constitution of 1940 concerning the role of the government in controlling not only the amount of land for each type of productive enterprise, but the entire agricultural system—"shall regulate by administration" (Article 275)—the very least that can be said is that Castro's 1953 idea of *direction* is an unknown quantity. Certainly the American experience proves once and for all that men who hold title to their farms can be directed to an extensive degree by the government. At this point, therefore, it would seem clear that the speech reveals in connection with agriculture (and cooperatives per se) the same kind of tension that characterizes Castro's discussion of other issues and subjects.

The second relevant consideration involves the way that Draper is prone to criticize other commentators on the Revolution because they fail to quote a remark by Castro (or one of his close advisors) that he chooses to emphasize in his interpretation. There is nothing reprehensible in that, particularly if the neglected source turns out to be pertinent. But in this instance (and there are others) it is Draper who fails to note an item that throws considerable light on the very issue he is discussing. He knows this, moreover, because he talks around it on several occasions.

Early in 1957, while he and the members of the original July 26th Movement were struggling to survive in the mountains, Castro wrote a book called *Revolución*. It was an essay in definition and defense of the revolution he was waging, and was clearly intended to win some of the help that Castro so obviously needed. Since he knows the volume, it is particularly disturbing that Draper does not quote from it, either in framing his bill of particulars for indicting Castro for betraying the Revolution, or in connection with this specific question about Castro's outlook on agriculture. Here is the pertinent passage: "The Revolution is struggling for a total transformation of Cuban life, for profound modifications in the system of property and for a change in institutions. . . . The Revolution is democratic, nationalist, and socialist."

It would be just as much of a mistake to read this passage as previewing all that has happened in Cuba since 1959 as to ignore it completely. For one thing, Castro said later in 1957, and again in 1958, that he had reconsidered and modified his views on nationalization as a technique of development. Even more importantly, Castro's socialism of early 1957 was the programmatic, stereotyped kind of socialism so typical of those who have just become favorably aware of the philosophy. It was the socialism of a man searching for a way to lift the reality of Cuban life up to the level of its potentialities.

It was the socialism, finally, of a man committed to the Cuban Constitution of 1940 and perplexed and troubled by the tensions and demands of that document. To understand this, one has to realize that inherent in the Constitution was a brain- and heart-breaker of a challenge. A commitment to that instrument of government could be honored, at least in theory, *and in its directives concerning domestic affairs,* by moving along one of three courses of action. First, a benevolent despot backed by a strong political-military organization involving some support from the lower class could probably manipulate the system of representative government to retain power indefinitely while he reconstructed the economic system along state capitalist lines. Second, a political organization advocating a corporate state could win control of the government and proceed with a similar program. If built upon strength in the middle and lower classes (as well as among the more perceptive members of the upper class), as Batista apparently had in mind in the mid-1930's, such a party might win elections for a generation or more. Finally, the domestic provisions of the Constitution could be honored by a radical bourgeois or socialist movement.

But, and this is the key point, only a radical bourgeois or socialist movement would be predisposed and willing to break the power of the United States in Cuba. Yet the drastic reduction of that American power, and a fundamental transformation of the character and the spirit of what remained, was the prerequisite to putting the domestic provisions of the Constitution into operation. For that matter, such a reduction of American power was an explicit directive in the Constitution itself. Read the document either way, in its implicit logical demands or in its specific demands, and the conclusion is the same. The Cuban Constitution of 1940 could not in fact be honored unless the existing pattern of American control of the island was changed into an entirely different kind of relationship.

That was the wrenching challenge that Castro had confronted since 1953. But here is the real importance of the passage from *Revolución* that Draper does not choose to print. *Castro never repudiated his commitment to "a total transformation of Cuban life, for profound modifications in the system of property and for a change in institutions."* Furthermore, he could not do so and still honor his pledge to the Constitution itself. Castro's actions on that commitment during the first six to seven months of his government were decisive, and need therefore to be reviewed with care.

7

The Crisis of the Revolution

*I. The Nature and Early
Development of the Crisis*

Alternate interpretations of the Cuban Revolution have thus far been kept before the reader to provide a continuing basis of evaluation. In considering the crucial period from January 1 through the promulgation (May 17) and the implementation (June 3) of the Agrarian Reform Law, and the initial reaction to that legislation, it is again useful to have such grounds for comparison.

Draper employs two arguments in making his interpretation. "The crisis," he writes in combining them, "came from within Castro's own 26th of July Movement and had been brewing from his first month in power. It was generated not by the United States but by the Communists, or rather by their sponsors and protectors in the Cuban Government." The point of decision, he adds somewhat later, was reached and passed "long before any overt American action was taken against the Castro regime."[1] In other commentary, he remarks that "the Castro regime was mainly concerned with maneuvering the United States into an unfavorable position."

The first and central weakness of Draper's analysis is that it breaks apart and polarizes two inter-related features of the crisis, and then arbitrarily discounts and ignores one of them. Part of the crisis did originate within the Castro government. Draper is correct to that extent. Its source was not the Communists (or their sponsors and protectors), however, but the nature of the Revolution and the dilemma inherent in its com-

---

1. The reader may recall that Draper says nothing of the Pawley maneuver of December, 1958.

mitment to the Constitution of 1940. This point Draper misses entirely, and his interpretation is therefore fundamentally mistaken.

Draper is also wrong, and very misleading, when he dismisses American policy on the grounds that it did not generate the crisis. Here is a classic example of how a proposition can be stated in such a way as to appear to be literally true and at the same time be in fact substantively false. Considered in the context of American-Cuban relations since 1895, and particularly after 1932, American policy did generate the crisis.

Looked at in the narrower sense, involving only relations after Castro came to power, the Draper proposition is still wrong because it is based on asking the wrong kind of question. Neither the historical nor the analytical problem is defined by a need to find *the* cause of the crisis, but rather by a need to see how the three major causes interacted with and upon each other. Thus the relevant question concerns the interplay between, on the one hand, the long- and short-run American policies and Castro's revolutionary commitment to the Constitution and, on the other hand, the tension and conflict within the revolutionary coalition over that commitment. As for the third factor, the existing and deepening economic crisis in Cuba, Draper ignores it completely. Yet this played a central role in the crisis of the Revolution.

One last point needs to be made in connection with the foreign policy part of Draper's analysis. His remark about "overt action" by the United States is misleading because it defines the issue in an artificial way. His formulation implies that overt acts are the only kind that influence people or events. But it ought to be apparent, even on the basis of daily personal experience, that passive behavior is often as damaging as overt action. It can be even more so. The failure to do something is as powerful a weapon of opposition or subversion as the violent maneuver. Psychologists have a term for it—passive-aggressive conduct. Benjamin Franklin's famous little paragraph makes the point even more appropriately: "A little neglect may breed mischief: for want of a nail the shoe was lost; for want of a shoe the horse was lost; and for want of a horse the rider was lost."

American policy from January 1 to July 1, 1959, clearly exerted considerable pressure on the Castro government and the Revolution. For that matter, and even discounting the Pawley gambit of December, 1958, some of the maneuvers by American officials came very close to being overt acts even by Draper's standards. The long delay in naming and sending Ambassador Bonsal provides such an example. Adolf A. Berle has offered an accurate and telling judgment on American policy in this period of crisis. "For a substantial period of time, the aggregate morale of the Cuban revolution was democratic, anti-dictatorial, and anti-Communist." It "could and should have been encouraged, canalized, and in the hour of its success, given very assistance."

It was not. And that failure of American policy exerted an ever more significant influence on the Revolution. Draper (and Meyer and Szulc as well) is wrong in asserting that Castro "was mainly concerned with maneuvering the United States into an unfavorable position." Castro was mainly concerned with carrying through a social revolution that was intimately interconnected with his commitment to the Constitution of 1940.

In embarking upon that effort, Castro moved first to provide the Cuban people with tangible benefits. More than a quarter of a million dollars was promptly invested in housing projects, schools, recreation facilities, and various other public works. Many of them were opened to the public within a month after Batista was defeated. Many salaries were raised. Electric power rates were cut. More telephones became available at lower cost. Rents were decreased as much as 50 percent on a $100 unit. Mortgage rates were reduced. And the price of meat was lowered.

Castro also launched a tax reform program to introduce more equity into the system, and to rationalize the collection of revenues. He hoped in this way to increase the amount of capital available to the government for its revolutionary program. One episode connected with this tax program may almost be said to symbolize the whole dynamic interaction between Castro and American business interests in Cuba. In order fully to savor it, however, some background is necessary.

The existing depression began immediately to influence the Cuban Revolution. Some of the unemployed that the Revolution inherited from Batista, and from the structurally unbalanced relations with the United States, were given jobs on the early public works projects. But that employment barely eased the situation. Over half a million Cubans were still out of work.

On February 11, 1959, Castro took other measures to cope with the difficulty. The government established control over imports, and increased its authority over foreign exchange transactions, in order to conserve capital. No restrictions were placed on the freedom of American companies to transfer their profits taken on operations in Cuba to their accounts in the United States. Speaking candidly of the increasing economic pressure on the Revolution, Castro concurrently asked various Cuban and American companies to advance part of their anticipated tax payments to help meet the crisis. Some of them cooperated. One of the deep ironies of the whole affair is that if the American government had followed the lead of these corporations, then the subsequent crisis might have been very much milder.

In the same period, as part of the tax reform program, the government requested American firms to present a new valuation of their property. Since it was no secret that Cuba's reform was aimed in part at the way corporations had evaded excess profit taxes, it may be presumed that the companies responded to the request with that dreary prospect in mind. In any event, they fudged the evidence (by lowering their property values) so as to gain at one end at least part of what they expected to lose at the other. The government accepted the figures as given. It also used them some time later as the basis for computing values in the course of nationalizing the investments.

During the crucial interval between the cheating and the expropriation, the continuing depression intensified all of Castro's problems and dilemmas. He spoke vividly in February of "the principal point of our economic program—industrialization at the fastest possible rate"—but it was almost impossible to locate the capital necessary for such an undertaking. It should not be forgotten, in this connection, that Castro did *not* initially embark upon a program of forced industrialization financed by the tired muscles and weary souls of Cuban workers. He instead gave priority to projects that improved the substance and tone of Cuba's immediate reality.

Given that set of priorities, the depression blocked any significant diversification of the economy through industrialization. The government did start a few small projects, such as a plant to process tomatoes in Cuba instead of selling them to the United States as a raw material and then buying the catchup as an import from Heinz. These operations were obviously symbolic. But the symbolism involved more than diversification through industrialization. It also caught the determination to rectify the unbalanced economic relationship with America's industrial power. The Cubans understood how the high-sounding principle of reciprocity treaties worked in practice quite as well as did Secretary of State Cordell Hull and his American successors. The Cubans merely learned the lesson from the other end of the empire.

Both in this sense, and in the one involving Castro's commitment to the Constitution of 1940, the inability to launch a significant program of industrialization increased Castro's difficulties in sustaining the élan and the momentum of the Revolution. This had two extremely important subsidiary consequences.

First, it put Castro in a very tight squeeze on the matter of policy toward the United States. On the one hand, he needed a minimum amount of short-term aid to tide Cuba over its immediate economic troubles. This point had been acknowledged by leaders of the Revolution as early as January. On the other hand, asking for such aid involved postponing action on the constitutional provisions respecting Cuba's economic sovereignty, involved a kind of emotional and idealistic surrender, and involved the risk of slowing the basic drive to transform Cuban society by tying the Revolution to the kind of preconditions that were part of the loan to Argentina.

All of this tension was openly revealed in Castro's remarks of February 20, 1959. He admitted again that the Revolution needed some aid. But he was aware that such grants seemed always to come at the price of limits set on what was being done inside the country that received them. The United States, he then observed, had been "interfering in Cuban affairs for more than fifty years." The time had come for Cuba "to solve its own problems." To illustrate the point, Castro pointed to the continuing remarks in the Congress, and elsewhere in the United States, about disciplining the Revolution through changes in the sugar quota.[1]

Castro's answer—"Cuba will sell sugar to anyone who has the money to buy it"—has to be considered in several dimensions. It was in the first place a manifestation of the nationalism so generally (and intensely) characteristic of all postwar revolutions in formerly colonial or neo-colonial societies. For Cuba, this assertiveness was as inherently anti-American as Egypt's was anti-British. One may not like this, but it will not do to argue that Cuba should overlook 63 years of American dominance. That is like saying that life begins at 64 after breaking com-

---

1. To say that Castro should not have been concerned with such talk is to step into intellectual quicksand. Such a remark implies that public discussion between officials, and in the mass media, has no effect on policy decisions in the United States. To say that is to say that there is no meaningful representative government in America.

pletely with the past—including an abandonment of social security and other retirement benefits.

Secondly, Castro was not suggesting some new and unheard-of proposals. Cuba had sold sugar to countries other than the United States for many years, and had always been concerned to enlarge its market. In view of declining commodity prices, Cuba would have to sell more sugar merely to maintain its existing income from that source. Castro had already mentioned, moreover, the idea of a vast expansion of sugar sales through which the Revolution could earn capital for diversification in agriculture and for industrialization.

Finally, Castro's remark was the reply in kind of a man who was being repeatedly thumped on a sore and delicate spot. Sugar was the key to Cuba's existing economy. Castro knew that as well as any economic expert, and the depression and his desire to diversify the economy intensified his awareness of the fact.

By the end of February, Castro was thus admitting that the Revolution was suffering in an economic embrace that was anything but pleasant. The two jaws of this vise were defined by the economic depression and the dependence on sugar. The pressure they exerted produced political as well as economic difficulties. And those in turn pushed Castro ever closer to the moment when he would have to decide what kind of compromise to strike between his need for capital and his commitment to a social revolution. Given the capital, Castro could carry through the Revolution and sustain the coalition. Without the capital, he had either drastically to modify both the nature and the tempo of the Revolution or antagonize (and lose) large segments of the coalition.

This was not an abstract issue. By the end of March, 1959, Castro was aware that even the first, moderate reforms had produced a significant weakening of the Revolutionary coalition of July, 1958. Draper is explicit and accurate in his description of this coalition: It "was never homogeneous, and the larger it grew in 1957 and 1958, the less homogeneous it became. It included those who merely wished to restore the Constitution of 1940 and those who demanded 'a real social revolution'."[1]

This being the case, Draper is wrong by his own evidence concerning his assertion that the Cuban middle class was "ready for deep-going social and political reforms." For, as he says, those "formerly pro-Castro middle-class adherents and sympathizers divided so much." Thus he is quite misleading when he goes on to say, in one of the crucial points in his interpretation, that "the 'moderates' did not 'abandon' the revolution; they were forced out."

Now in point of fact there is contemporary evidence dating from as early as April 4, 1959, that the moderates were beginning to oppose Castro. In her despatch of that date to the *New York Times,* for example, Ruby Hart Phillips spoke openly of such antagonism. Subsequent reports verified her first analysis. There was "uncertainty" in various segments of the coalition: the early and moderate reforms "have dismayed the conservatives and middle-of-the-roaders." Such elements did not like the new, lower interest rates on mortgages, the rent reductions, and the attention being given to the lower orders. And disturbed by American threats concerning the sugar quota, on which they based their well-being and position in Cuban society, they wanted Castro to come to terms with the United States.

Members of the "middle class," Mrs. Phillips noted, "are losing their enthusiasm for the revolution." These Cubans were not content with grumbling among themselves, or with verbal sallies against Castro. They increased the economic pressure on the Revolution by sitting on their capital. "Money has

---

1. It should be apparent that those Cubans described by Draper as wishing "merely . . . to restore the Constitution" wanted to restore it on a highly selective and limited basis.

tightened and no investments are being made." In particular, the building industry entered a recession that was caused by such political and social motivations on the part of Cuban entrepreneurs.

These activities—verbal, political, and economic—enable us to evaluate Draper's remark about the moderates. His formulation and language combine to create the impression that the radicals evicted the moderates from the coalition in a wholly unilateral action initiated without any reason. Now it is true that the moderates and conservatives ultimately lost; but they lost only after they became critical and only after they attempted to assert their power and control within the revolutionary coalition.

Draper's argument in some respects does such men a serious injustice. He presents them as passive victims. Actually, they honored their own upper- and middle-class values and ideas by fighting Castro's radicalism; they were defeated, but they did not hop off to Miami at the first bit of rough political weather. Some were torn, as Nicolas Rivero has remarked with candor and dignity, in "a psychological conflict between my ideological identification with the aims of the revolution and my family ties." Others were simply against the Revolution that Castro was trying to carry through. And some simply did not want to risk losing what they had.

But there is nothing novel or insidious about all this. Nor is there anything about it that makes it part of something that Draper calls "the Communist family" of revolutions. All revolutions are made by coalitions which become involved in militant internal struggles. This has nothing to do with a Communist pattern as against some other prototype. The phenomenon was as characteristic of the American Revolution as of the Bolshevik Revolution.

Some factions lose, others win. Those who lose either adapt to the new situation or leave—voluntarily or under duress. A historian may identify with the defeated, but his sympathies should not lead him to treat the battle as something which occurs only in a system he dislikes. To say merely that his favorites are driven out is to tell but half the story. It still takes two to tangle—even in Cuba.

The central question in connection with the Cuban example concerns the way in which the struggle developed once the moderates began to react against Castro's early reforms. And that in turn can be understood only in terms of Castro's attempt to break free of his central dilemma.

8

The Crisis of the Revolution

*II.   Castro's Strategy to Resolve the Crisis
and Sustain the Coalition*

Not too surprisingly, particularly so soon after the events themselves, all the facts essential to a full, detailed analysis of the crisis are simply not available. There is enough information, however, to rectify at the outset one of the most general errors that have been made in existing interpretations of the Revolution. This involves two seemingly disparate events: Castro's visit to the United States beginning April 15, and his appearance and speech on May 2, 1959, before the Sixth Plenary Session of the Economic Council of the Organization of American States meeting in Buenos Aires. These were not unconnected actions. They were the crucial moves in Castro's original effort to resolve the basic dilemma of the Revolution and must be considered as part of the same operation.

Let us again explicitly define Castro's central difficulty. He was a radical revolutionary at the head of a coalition which included many moderates and some conservatives. The moderates and conservatives had by the end of March, 1959, begun to oppose even the modest reforms enacted up to that point. They had, by their economic actions, intensified an existing economic depression. Yet Castro was determined to carry through the Revolution to which he was committed—both in general and by his pledge to the Constitution of 1940—by industrial diversification and by executing a fundamental agrarian reform. He clearly hoped to do this without losing the basic support of the moderate elements in the revolutionary coalition.

The only way that Castro could reconcile those conflicting factors was by obtaining capital on terms that did not abort the revolutionary program to which he was committed. Such aid was the only thing that would enable him to honor his commitment to the Constitution of 1940 without at the same time demanding extensive sacrifices from the Cuban population, and without disrupting the revolutionary coalition.

Castro said much of this, and implied the rest, in the course of an interview printed in *U.S. News and World Report* on March 16, 1959. Asked to describe the fundamental problem facing the Revolution, Castro replied that "it is as if we had been fenced in for many decades." The long-range problem was to free Cuba from its peonage to sugar. This meant starting consumer industries, but that was impossible "unless there is purchasing power." Castro then turned to the existing economic crisis. "Our big problem is the hundreds of thousands of men who are out of work." His concern with that difficulty was again dramatized, near the end of the conversation, when he was asked about revolutionary support for the opponents of dictators in other Latin American countries. Castro admitted he would like to see them deposed. But he added a revealing *caveat*: "What worries me in these moments are the problems of Cuba."

In between these crucial remarks, the magazine reporter asked Castro a pointed question about what he meant by industrialization. What kind of industries? "Principally those," he replied, "that produce foods, a textile industry and industries to produce manufactured products for Cuban consumption." Castro then explained the connection between agricultural reform and such industrialization, and why the former had to be initiated before the latter. "The agrarian reform will increase many times the purchasing power of the farmer, and it will be the base for industrial development in Cuba."

Finally, the discussion turned to the delicate but fundamental question concerning the sources of capital for the combined program. Castro's answer revealed the way that he hoped to resolve the dilemma of obtaining capital without paying an exorbitant political as well as economic price. "Fundamentally," he explained, "we want to have capital loaned to us so that we can invest it through the credit agencies of the country, because, if capital comes from abroad and is invested directly, we have to pay interest, which is the cost of the capital, we have to amortize the capital, yet after we have amortized it we have nothing."

Castro's remarks may appear to be somewhat confused; he was talking in a compressed and short-hand way about several problems connected with obtaining capital for underdeveloped countries. But the cryptic nature of his reply is significant in itself because it indicates how much thinking Castro and his associates had been doing in connection with the problem and how to solve it. A general review of the subject will help clarify his meaning.

There are four basic ways in which a developing country can obtain aid from the United States:

The first involves private investment. With the approval and collaboration, or at least the acquiescence, of the developing country, foreign entrepreneurs undertake to exploit resources, provide manufacturing plants, or to supply services. This can be done by a branch of the American corporation (direct investment), or indirectly by having American operators supply capital and assistance of other kinds for projects undertaken by Cubans (portfolio investment or simple loans). At best, the Castro government would exercise some initial measure of authority over such operations; it might, for example, approve the undertakings according to some set of priorities it established. Even there, however, considerable restraint would be necessary to avoid antagonizing American capitalists.

Beyond that first check, Cuba would not enjoy much control over the functioning of those units in the economy *unless it nationalized them or in some other way exerted its legitimate power as defined in the Constitution of 1940.* In the meantime, the Cuban economy would be paying interest without buying

93

any control over the facilities. And if it nationalized them, no more private capital would be forthcoming. It may very well be, for that matter, that the sharp drop in American investments which took place as soon as Castro came to power (and *before* he nationalized the American sector of the economy) was the direct result of a fear that Castro meant exactly what he said about the Constitution of 1940. It is wise to remember in this connection that *Business Week* was the only magazine in the United States to give any attention to the Constitution when it went into operation.

The Export-Import Bank is a second source of capital. Originally designed to finance the export of American surpluses during the Great Depression, the Bank began near the end of the 1930's to underwrite various public works projects that were seen to be necessary if the underdeveloped countries in Latin America were ever to provide a steady and expanding market for exports from the United States. Roads, shipping facilities, and other transportation and communications installations, sanitation projects, and power supplies were included in this general expansion of the Bank's operations.

Such improvements are of course essential not only for the American economic system to tie in and function profitably with the economy of the developing country (how sell toasters without electricity or cars without roads?), but also for the improvement of the poor country per se. Here again, however, the poor country pays interest in dollars and in politics, even though few of the projects ever provide effective levers by which it can control or direct the shape of its own future development.

A third general approach involves government to government loans in one of many forms. These loans usually involve various terms which, from the point of view of a government like Castro's, severely limit their usefulness. Many of them, for example, involve the construction of facilities which are ultimately turned over to private entrepreneurs. Others are granted to meet existing debts, or to refund them, and carry as part of their price tag specific provisos concerning interest rates, price levels, import and exchange controls, and other limitations which impinge directly upon (and throughout) the political economy of the poor country.

None of these kinds of loans squared with the Cuban Constitution of 1940. And, in one way or another, they all carried stipulations that would have seriously restricted Castro's ability to carry through on his revolutionary program. Castro needed straight economic loans, either from private firms or from governments. In an ironic way, he wanted to operate on the basis of Calvin Coolidge's wry comment about "hiring the money." Castro wanted to hire the money, use it to direct the development of the Cuban economy in accordance with the Constitution of 1940 and his own revolutionary program, and then have that system stand free of outside control when the money was repaid. This may have been one of Castro's petty bourgeois prejudices, but it was the basis of his approach to the problem.

In theory, and as suggested by the foregoing review of American loan practice, Castro could obtain capital from several sources. Private investment bankers, either in the United States or in Western Europe, could provide some of it. But only a portion. An international syndicate might conceivably underwrite a large part of his entire program for Cuban development, but such consortiums were not usually keen on that kind of project. In any case, individual banks, or such a consortium, would undoubtedly make certain conditions for the loan; and, even if they were general in nature, Castro would lose some—or all—of the economic and political margin of safety he needed to carry through his plans.

Government loans offered another option. In practice, however, this road led only to the United States. Western European countries were not making many advances of that kind in 1959, and none of them were apt to risk offending the United States by appearing to challenge the American position.

But a loan from the United States would sustain and probably reinforce the existing tradition of authority over the island's affairs. It was thus the least attractive possibility.

Castro's final choice involved obtaining assistance from one of the international lending agencies. In reality, however, he was limited to three institutions: the United Nations Special Fund for Economic Development, the World Bank, or the International Monetary Fund. But the UN source did not have much working capital, and its entire operation had been severely restricted by American reservations and outright opposition. For both reasons, the SUNFED operation did not hold much promise for Castro.

Similar considerations were involved in dealing with the other two banks. While they are not formal agencies of the United States Government, and even make a fuss periodically about their independence, both the World Bank and the International Monetary Fund are routinely subject to great American influence. Sometimes this is direct and obvious, as when a key American leader holds the top executive position; at other times the power is exerted more indirectly. Neither institution makes loans against the strong opposition of the United States. Nor has either been noted for fulsome help to radical reconstructions of the status quo. There exists, nevertheless, the possibility that they will consider, and ultimately authorize, a grant that is questionable from the American point of view.

Castro recognized these more favorable aspects of dealing through those institutions, estimated the odds, and chose to approach the International Monetary Fund for the kind of a loan he wanted and needed to carry through his revolutionary program. The details of this request and the subsequent negotiations are not clear. The episode has been referred to in general terms by several men, among them Rufo López Fresquet, Felipe Pazos, and Nicolas Rivero, who during the spring of 1959 held official positions in the coalition governing Cuba. But none of these men has provided anything approaching a clear, straightforward story of the negotiations.

It seems wise, before reviewing the course of those discussions, to consider the possibility that Castro's idea of an acceptable loan was so unreasonable or unprofessional that there was no reason to take it seriously. The main weakness in that line of argument is that Pazos proposed the same approach over a year before Castro came to power, and Pazos is recognized as an exceptionally able and responsible economic expert and administrator. His performance as President of the National Bank of Cuba, for example, has been praised by men of widely different political views.

Pazos made his recommendation at the end of a long, detailed, and brilliant paper, "Private Versus Public Foreign Investment in Under-Developed Areas," which he presented in 1957 to a conference of Western Hemispheric economic leaders. It was finally printed in 1961 as part of the proceedings of the conference in a volume edited by Howard S. Ellis and Henry C. Wallich: *Economic Development for Latin America*. Pazos buttressed his own analysis and argument for such loans by reference to the earlier study prepared in 1954 by the United Nations: *Economic Cooperation in a Latin American Development Policy*. It would seem apparent, therefore, that Castro's concept of the right kind of loan was anything but wild or irresponsible.

There is even more to this part of the story. Castro's basic definition of the desirable kind of loan, which he provided in his March, 1959, interview with the reporter from *U.S. News and World Report*, bears a striking similarity in phrasing as well as substance to the remarks by Pazos in his paper of 1957. This suggests two things: (1) that Castro learned (or borrowed) the idea from Pazos; and (2) that Castro tried to hold out for the best type of loan, whereas Pazos proved willing to accept the kind of loan he admitted was inferior on political as well as economic grounds.

These facts and considerations also bear directly on the existing accounts of Castro's negotiations for a loan. As told by Pazos, Fresquet, and Rivero (and repeated by Draper and other American critics of Castro), the point of the story is to show that Castro did not really want a loan and that he did not make any serious effort to obtain one. They imply even more— that both the United States and the International Monetary Fund were eager to extend generous assistance. Such a telling of the story is misleading as well as vague and cryptic. Castro is not credited with taking the initiative, nor is anything said about the conditions upon which the aid was being offered. Yet these were the central points at issue. This is like saying that a man refused the offer of a loan to build the home of his dreams without adding that he had applied for the assistance only to find that, as a condition of the loan, the plans would have to be altered, and that the interest was to be 10 percent compounded semi-annually.

It is not necessary, however, to rely so exclusively on such partial accounts of the episode. Further evidence is available. American newspapers carried reports of the bid by Castro at the time it was being made. These make it clear that the men in Castro's government, all of whom later joined the opposition to Castro, are not telling the whole story. This additional evidence also disproves Draper's claim that "Castro did not even wish to try" for such economic aid.

Finally, I may report on my own persistent efforts to uncover still further information. The resulting evidence is largely indirect, but it is no less revealing for that. On the basis of the published data, and with the assistance of various people, including government officials of no mean influence, I asked the International Monetary Fund a straightforward question: Did Castro initiate discussions for a loan and, if so, what was the course of the negotiations and the grounds for the final termination of the talks? The International Monetary Fund spokesmen first evaded the question. Then they refused to discuss the matter further. The following reconstruction of what happened is based, therefore, on the evidence discovered (and cross-checked) in an extensive search of published materials. It is not offered as a definitive account, only as a more accurate one than those in existence, and is of course subject to modification when further verified information becomes available.

Considerable data on the matter appeared in various news despatches datelined April 22, 1959, after Castro left Washington for New York. One story revealed that Castro had first approached the International Monetary Fund "several weeks ago." On the same day, Castro made a remark in New York that was typical of many he uttered during this crisis period of the Revolution, and which cast additional light on the item about the dealings with the International Monetary Fund. Asked whether he expected a large loan, he replied negatively: "first, because we do not want it and, second, because we could not get it."

Given the context of the remark, and understanding Castro's broad dilemma, no special training in psychology is needed to see the combination of pride, frustration, worry, and inside knowledge that produced the two contradictory halves of Castro's answer. Draper and other commentators have nevertheless chosen to take such remarks with a brittle literalness which enables them to argue that Castro (and other Cuban leaders such as Guevara) did not want aid, or even the American market for Cuban sugar. But the true meaning of Castro's comment is both more complex and rather different.

In the first place, there was no reason for Castro to raise the point about not being able to obtain a loan if he was actually disinterested. And he had never said flatly, once and for all, that the revolutionary government did not want any kind of economic assistance. All his remarks prior to April 22, and for some time thereafter, contain an inherent and obvious tension between the need for such aid and the troubles and restrictions involved in meeting or satisfying the need. If Castro was trying simply and only to put the United States in an unfavorable light, as so many commentators insist, then he would have concentrated on the inability of the Revolution to secure a loan. He did not. One final point is noteworthy in this connection: the United States has never chosen to integrate and emphasize the charge that he refused help into its increasingly bitter attacks on Castro. Surely it would have done so if the facts were as simple and as pat as they are implied to be by the exiles, and others who rely upon that evidence.

Castro in his remarks of April 22, 1959, was in one sense disparaging such loans simply because he was in a very tight corner and did in fact need and want such aid very much indeed. Most human beings have a propensity to react that way under such conditions. Many less volatile than Castro indulge the urge. He was also torn between that need and his understanding (and resultant fear) of the kind of stipulations that would be included in the price for the money. And finally, he very probably knew on April 22 that such conditions had already been raised in the negotiations with the International Monetary Fund, and was saying that Cuba could not get a loan simply because that happened to be the case.

This reading of those two news stories of April 22 is borne out by three other pieces of evidence. First, Castro was very explicitly trying to use his visit to the United States as a means of building general support in the circles that do exert a measure of influence on official American policy. He was in this sense going to the people over the head of the official bankers in an effort to win popular backing—or at least sympathy—for more generous terms. Castro explained this very candidly a short time later during his attendance at the Organization of American States meeting in Buenos Aires.

Next, and more explicitly, a story in the *New York Times* of April 26 revealed that there had been two rounds of talks between Cuba and the International Monetary Fund. The reason that no loan had been forthcoming was most revealing:

"the Castro Government has not shown itself prepared yet to accept a stabilization program." If in no other way, Castro had gained a clear picture of the results of such a stabilization program through the example offered by Argentina during December, 1958, and January, 1959. The terms of that loan had exerted tremendous and immediate pressures on the lower classes, and had thereby provoked serious social and political unrest. Even if Castro had been willing to risk such short-run consequences, which he most certainly could not afford to do in view of Cuba's existing 700,000 unemployed, he could not take comfort in the thought that such stipulations were designed to facilitate and ease the course of a thoroughgoing social revolution such as he was trying to effect. Hardly. The whole point of the stabilization program was to prevent such revolutions. From either angle, the short-run or the long-term, Castro could not be expected to agree to securing the loan he needed by accepting conditions that subverted the purpose of the loan itself.

Finally, an especially keen despatch of April 22, 1959, by Edwin W. Kenworthy of the *New York Times* made it perfectly apparent that the United States Government understood Castro's dilemma, and that it was knowingly exerting pressure on him. Kenworthy based his story on talks with government economists and other officials concerned with the Cuban issue. The economists agreed that the Cuban depression was the key to the entire situation. They were also candid in saying that Castro had inherited the problem from Batista; and, in the broader sense, that it was caused by the unbalanced relation between Cuba and the United States and the general decline in commodity prices. The depression "is not of Dr. Castro's making, in the opinion of economists here," Kenworthy reported, "and would have hit the Government of President Fulgencio Batista." This analysis is also supported by the testimony of Rivero, who was very concerned to use Castro's visit to the United States to win an increase in the sugar quota, and to obtain a loan, in order to deal with the depression.

Castro could "limp along a few more months," the American officials admitted, "but a day of decision is coming." They predicted that point would be reached in October or November. Castro would then have to make up his mind about coming to terms with the United States for a loan. Kenworthy described the choice very clearly: "If Dr. Castro is to get large-scale aid for his . . . problems, he will have to agree to a stabilization program. . . . This would chiefly involve credit restraint and a balanced—or nearly balanced budget." If he refused to accept those conditions, a government economist commented, then Castro "will have to adopt a controlled economy."

It is thus clear that American officials saw and understood the crisis of the Revolution. Castro could obtain aid, but only by acquiescing in terms that would prevent him from carrying through the social revolution by denying him the use of the tool of deficit financing for handling industrialization and agrarian reform, and by imposing economic controls that would be very apt to stir popular unrest against his government. The stabilization conditions, in other words, were basically designed to preserve the Cuban status quo, allowing only a few fringe reforms to be put into operation. If, on the other hand, Castro chose to go ahead with the Revolution, then he would have to subject the Cuban people to severe pressures and hardships. One economist put the point bluntly: "Castro will either have to come over in our direction, or go in the direction of Argentina during the latter years of Peron's regime."

Though they agreed on a broad analysis of the existing crisis, and on the choices open to Castro, American officials divided over the proper policy for the United States to follow in the months ahead. The option, as Kenworthy explained, was reasonably clear: "Whether to sit back and await developments—'to let the Castro Government go through the wringer,' as one official put it—or to take the initiative by manifesting a willingness to give aid upon Cuba's agreement to a stabilization program."

Some American officials favored letting Castro "go through the wringer." This meant that they were willing to force the Cuban people to go along on the ride. Others, Kenworthy reported, "strongly advise that the United States take the initiative." In their view, the wringer approach would produce a dictator, or would give the Cuban Communist Party an excellent opportunity to exert great influence on the Revolution.

This one news story by Kenworthy throws a vast amount of very bright light on the entire development of the Cuban Revolution, and especially on American policy during the crisis period of January to July, 1959:

First, it suggests very strongly that the offers of American aid reported by various Cubans were contingent upon the acceptance by Castro of a stabilization program similar to the one imposed upon Argentina.

Second, it reinforces the evidence that the same demand brought an end to Cuba's discussions with the International Monetary Fund.

Third, it establishes beyond any question that the United States was exerting pressure on Castro's Revolution *before* the promulgation of the Agrarian Reform Law.

Fourth, it demonstrates conclusively that the United States was willing to subject the Cuban people to further hardships in order to enforce its own demand for a stabilization program as the price of a loan.

Fifth, it is likewise clear that the United States in exerting this pressure knew that it was offering Castro a choice that was not a choice. The American proposition, along with the one offered by the International Monetary Fund, involved telling Castro that he could have a loan if he gave up the social revolution to which he was committed.

Sixth, and finally, it is manifest that the United States government held to that condition even though some of its experts saw—and specified very precisely—the dangerous consequences that were very apt to occur if Castro refused to surrender his commitment to the Revolution despite the American pressure.

Castro very probably knew, or had strong intimations of, all these considerations by the time he left Washington. He nevertheless continued his efforts to gain support in the United States through a straightforward explanation and defense of the projected agrarian reform and other revolutionary programs. Though he continued to gain a hearing after he moved on from New York, Castro soon thereafter cut short his visit for a meeting with his brother Raúl in Houston to discuss conservative and Communist pressure on the revolutionary government during his absence, and to fly on to an important OAS conference in Buenos Aires.

Despite the confident tone of his public reports, Castro may have been discouraged by the results of his trip to the United States. American officials were correct but neither very sympathetic nor encouraging. Much has been made of President Eisenhower's failure to see Castro, and of the manner in which Secretary of State Christian Herter handled his meeting with Castro; but, while that criticism is relevant, it really misses the central point. It was the Congress, which had been antagonistic towards Castro from the outset, which actually took charge of the visit. The whole notion that Castro should appear before a select committee of Congressional leaders in order to satisfy their fears and apprehensions was a classic symbol of the basic nature of American policy toward Cuba since 1895. Castro won a rather reluctant and begrudging respect from most of the Congressmen, but very little—if any—active support. Other influential leaders, such as labor union officials, were very cool. He made a significant impression only among those who lacked any important short-run influence on policy makers.

Whatever his estimate of the chances—as contrasted with his hopes—that the United States would modify its attitude, Castro nevertheless carried his campaign for a loan to the OAS economic conference in Buenos Aires. His speech of May 2,

1959, was one of the most impressive performances of his entire career. It was restrained and generous toward the United States, and in form, substance, and style revealed that he had invested a great deal of thought in trying to work out a resolution of his central dilemma. Considered in the context of the Revolution up to that date, his remarks create (even three years later) a strong impression that the American trip was conceived and executed as a means to win a serious and successful hearing for the idea and program he laid before the delegates at Buenos Aires.

Castro opened his speech of May 2 in a way that revealed how intensely concerned he was about the political squeeze he faced in Cuba. He used his own experiences to make the point that all Latin American leaders who wanted to transform the region were confronted by the same dilemma—attacks from the extreme Right and the extreme Left. After lashing out at both kinds of tyranny, he proceeded to analyze the crisis and to offer a dramatic program whereby Latin America could have its revolution with a minimum of death, pain, and suffering— and with the fewest infringements on representative government and political freedom.

"The trouble," Castro began, "is fundamentally in our economic and social conditions. . . . All of us are conscious of our economic backwardness." He had continually discussed these matters during his recent visit to the United States, he explained, because the North Americans needed help in understanding and in coming to terms with the situation. "Latin America faces dangers that the United States does not face. We have problems that the United States does not have. In the United States, political stability is guaranteed by economic stability, together with other unique factors. Therefore it is sometimes difficult for the United States to understand the problem of Latin America."

Such understanding was nevertheless essential, and hence a continuing effort had to be made to bring reality to the attention of the North Americans. The United States dominated the hemisphere and it had to accept the responsibilities of its privileged position. Otherwise it was very unlikely that the crisis could be surmounted without producing tyrannies of the Left and Right. The solution was to modernize the economies of the region and thereby provide the fundamental stability that was a prerequisite of other advances. For Castro, at any rate, industrialization was the single most important phase of such development.

"We in Cuba are confronted with this problem and we know there is only one way to provide jobs for our 700 thousand unemployed."

"We are not going to give them worthless currency."

"Nor can we feed them air."

"And we are not going to employ them in some unproductive work tantamount to digging one hole to fill another."

Neither could it be done under the existing pattern and structure of trade: that "barely suffices to pay for the consumer goods we import and, in many instances, not even for that."

The accumulation of capital was the only effective answer to the problem; capital in large enough quantities, and under such terms, as to make it possible to carry through the agrarian and industrial reforms that would lift Cuba and other Latin American countries out of their neo-feudal past into the modern world. Having established his line of argument, Castro proceeded to outline and discuss the three principal ways of obtaining capital: by saving, through trade, and through loans.

While saving was in many instances an effective, even noble, method, it was either impractical or exceedingly dangerous for backward countries. They were poor and imbalanced to start with, and hence had no real reservoir of current profits which could be tapped for the kind of capital required to finance major changes and improvements. The wealthy might overcome their narrow interest-conscious outlook, revitalize the old Latin upper class tradition of *noblesse oblige,* and accept the responsibility for such development. Even under the best of circumstances, however, that would lead to a benevolent despotism of the Right. Given the inherent difficulties facing Latin American nations, it would produce a real tyranny very rapidly. The desperate obstacles to accumulating capital inside those countries would make it impossible to be benevolent. There was simply not enough wealth to underwrite the operation of that kind of system.

Castro was understandably more attracted by the possibility of financing development through increased trade. "If Cuba, for example, could sell eight million tons of sugar, we would be able to obtain the capital needed for our industrial development." He was not optimistic, however, about that possibility. It would require significant modifications in American trade policy. "But such changes would imply a change in the structure of the United States. I am not going to be Utopian." Castro understood that high-pressure tariff politics in the United States, combined with the system's reliance on exporting its surpluses, made it highly improbable that a genuine free trade policy would ever be adopted. "We are aware," he commented, "that such a change on a scale large enough really to allow a considerable increase in our exportation of primary products, would be one of the most difficult ways for the United States to cooperate with us."

That left loans as the only other source of capital. Castro first considered the difficulties involved in financing development through private investment. The foreigners who had such capital, he noted accurately enough, wanted what they termed "a favorable climate" for their operations in the poorer countries. They demanded, that is to say, government assistance to decrease the risks of their free enterprise, but not government action to lower the risks for the poorer society. American businessmen and officials presented a bipartisan phalanx on this issue: Secretary of State Dean Acheson emphasized it no less than Secretary Dulles.

In a series of remarks clearly based on Cuba's own experience with such private investment, and on his own understanding of the American stabilization programs designed to provide such a favorable climate, Castro explained why it was impossible to exercise that extensive a control over the social and political weather in the poorer countries. In the first place, the situation in underdeveloped or developing countries was inherently dynamic. People were expressing their dissatisfactions, acting to change the existing situation, and generally being uncooperative in creating a climate favorable for low-risk private investment. They could be controlled, but only in ways that produced the worst tyranny of all—tyranny for the convenience of foreigners.

Castro next explained—with a clear reference to the United States—why stabilization loans failed to solve the problem. And, finally, he pointed out that successful private investments only changed the form of the problem. Conflicts between capital and labor, for example, became international issues. That placed the government of the poorer country in a very difficult situation. Either it had to repress or subdue its own citizens in the name of stabilizing the climate for investment by foreigners, or it had to risk serious trouble with the government of the powerful industrial nation.

The implications were obvious: the only satisfactory way to obtain the necessary capital was through a massive and long-term loan from the United States. It had to be huge because all the countries in Latin America had to develop together. Otherwise the region would slip into the vicious pattern wherein the rich climbed higher and the poor sank lower. It had to be long-term because time was needed for development to occur. And it had to be a strictly business loan so that the Latin American countries could maintain and strengthen their sovereignty and independence, and so that they could carry out the drastic reforms that were needed.

Castro was trying very seriously and politely—but also very

directly—to help the United States see and understand and act upon a vital point. *There was no way to prevent revolutions in underdeveloped and developing countries; there were only ways to make them less costly, painful, or tyrannical.*

On the basis of this insight, Castro then asked the United States to loan Latin American countries a grand total of $30 billion repayable in 10 years. He admitted that this would require a new and significant sacrifice from the already generous and burdened American taxpayer. He very bluntly asked them to make it for two reasons: to help their fellow citizens of the Western Hemisphere, and to avoid forcing Latin Americans to choose between no (or terribly retarded) development and development under tyrannies of the Right and the Left.

Castro's speech of May 2, 1959, at Buenos Aires was sober, thoughtful, and tightly argued. Its only real weakness concerned the amount of capital that would be required. The sum he requested was very probably too small by half. Even so, his request was dismissed as ridiculous in the United States. Latin American leaders gave Castro a moving ovation at the end of his talk, but they also anticipated the signals of disapproval being hoisted in Washington. Castro acquiesced in the defeat and withdrew the plan to avoid an embarrassing—and painful —situation for all concerned.

To avoid a similar, and equally fruitless, exercise in hairsplitting, one may agree with Draper that up to this time the United States had not committed any overt act against Castro and the Cuban Revolution. It had merely decided to stand by and let both of them go through the wringer.

Accompanied by the Cuban people.

9

The Crisis of the Revolution
III. The Agrarian Reform Law and
Castro's First Calculated Risk

Upon his return to Cuba from his trips to the United States and the OAS economic conference in Buenos Aires, Castro immediately realized that the crisis of the Revolution had become significantly more serious during his absence. Conservatives, moderates, and Communists were attacking the government and its programs, and attempting to influence it overtly as well as implicitly. He faced this situation quite aware that he had very little chance to resolve the dilemma by obtaining capital on terms that would allow him to carry through the Revolution explicit in his own outlook and implicit in his commitment to the Cuban Constitution of 1940.

It can be maintained that, if there was a turning point in the Revolution, it came between Castro's return from Buenos Aires and his announcement of the Agrarian Reform Law on May 17, 1959. Actually, if one is going to discuss the Revolution in terms of turning points, then it is far more accurate to say that it came when the United States Government decided to let Castro "go through the wringer." But it can be argued, in an abstract sort of way, that Castro could have given in to the economic crisis, and retreated when confronted by conservative and Communist challenges to his leadership, struck a bargain with the moderates who were willing to meet American terms for a loan, and proceeded to carry through the modest reforms that would have been possible under those conditions.

It is possible to make this contention, either overtly or implicitly, as do Draper and other critics. But it is not very meaningful to do so because it is an assertion based on a high degree of abstraction: it treats Castro as though he were a consensus politician in the mold of Lyndon B. Johnson rather than a dedicated revolutionary. This can be done (and people who would like it to be true are prone to do it) but it has almost no relation to reality. Castro is a revolutionary committed to a program of radical reconstruction, and it is very doubtful whether it ever entered his mind to retreat from that position. And since *could* concerns ability, the argument is stronger as well as more candid when cast in terms of *should*. In terms, that is to say, of the preferences of the American (or other) critic.

As it happened, Castro moved first after his return to attack the Communist challenge to his leadership. He did so very bluntly and angrily on May 8 and 16, dissociating himself from the Communist Party and its ideas and programs. He subsequently acted in June to block Communist influence in the labor movement. Even before that, on May 26, the Communists made it clear that they had been hurt by Castro's open opposition. They attacked his leadership and claimed that the Revolution could not succeed without their support.[1]

Castro had meanwhile moved on to promulgate the Agrarian Reform Law on May 17, 1959. "We are only trying," he remarked in announcing the program, "to move from feudalism to enlightened capitalism." The law immediately provoked vigorous criticism from conservative and moderate Cubans, and from American sugar and other agricultural interests. Castro was adamant. "This is a necessary measure, a surgical operation," he angrily replied, "that must be carried out in the interest of the national economy." He also spoke at this time in very candid terms—contrary to what Draper and others have written—about the sacrifices and austerity that would be necessary in order to carry through this fundamental reorganization of the entire Cuban political economy.

---

1. On this point of Communist counterattacks, see the *New York Times* of May 26 and 27, 1959.

Since the law is central to an understanding of the Revolution, and because it has provoked so much bitter and distorted comment as well as opposition, it seems particularly useful—and sobering—to consider the judgment of Nicolas Rivero after he had left the government and supported the unsuccessful invasion of 1961. The reform, Rivero accurately explains, was the "turning point in the transformation of the social structure of Cuba." "The main objective of the Agrarian Reform Law," he continues (in agreement with part of Castro's own evaluation), "was to diversify agriculture in order to make Cuba less dependent on a one-crop economy and at the same time to establish a sound rural population that would create a potential market for the industrialization of the country."

Rivero is accurate but incomplete. A second, and equally important, objective of the agrarian reform is to transform the substance and the tone of life for the Cuban peasant (and, as a result, for all Cubans). The law cannot be understood, nor its impact comprehended, unless this point is grasped very firmly. It is a radical and revolutionary law in its social as well as its economic objectives. Castro indicated the intensity of his concern, and also revealed the extent of his identification with rural Cuba, in a later remark during a tour of various projects started under the law. "I'm more interested in chickens, sugar and agrarian reform than in the OAS." And pigs, he might have added, in view of his special interest in and knowledge of the subject of pork culture.

Castro's vigorous and assertive personal leadership in the writing of the Agrarian Reform Law was unquestionably an instance of quasi-dictatorial power. He overrode more moderate officials in the coalition government, and even some of his old and close colleagues in the original 26th July Movement. He was the premier, however, and the actual as well as the symbolic leader of the coalition that defeated Batista.

The premier has great authority and responsibility in such a system of government. Winston Churchill remarked with his characteristic bluntness, during a crisis within the Allied coalition of World War II, that—whatever the ideal politics of compromise—"somebody has to play the hand." This is as true of a revolutionary movement as it is of a wartime partnership. Something is assigned second place in the hierarchy of values in every political situation. In the politics of the Agrarian Reform Law, as in other crucial episodes including many in the United States, decision by vote within the cabinet took second place. Castro used his power and accepted responsibility for what he did with it.

The agrarian law that Castro drove through was designed to accomplish its objectives through five major provisions. Four of these were clearly demanded—let alone justified—by the Constitution of 1940.

First: the breaking-up of the old, quasi-feudal estate system of ownership and production in sugar (and in agriculture generally). Save in the cattle industry, where something over 3,000 acres was legalized, personal land holdings were limited to 1,000 acres.

Second: the breaking-up of the pattern of foreign power in the sugar industry. This was done by divorcing the production of sugar from the processing operation by requiring the latter to be handled by Cuban-owned corporations. In addition, of course, American economic power was undercut by the provisos concerning acreage.

Third: the redistribution of land to the Cuban peasant. Since American commentators have created the impression that this never occurred in fact, but only in Castro's rhetoric, it is worthwhile to quote Rivero on the issue. "It is true that with this agrarian reform a new class of private farmers has emerged in Cuba, most of whom once worked on someone else's land as planters, leasers, sharecroppers, or just squatters." And many others, who never enjoyed even those tenuous connections with the land, have also become private farmers.

Fourth: the diversification of Cuban agriculture through

the provisions of the Constitution concerning education, the modification of the dependence on sugar, and the direction of the economy per se.

Castro took the first of two crucial calculated risks of the Revolution in connection with the final major provision of the Agrarian Reform Law. This involved the nature and the role of cooperatives. The law specified that "whenever possible" the National Institute of Agrarian Reform "will promote agrarian cooperatives," and gave the Institute administrative control over such organizations "until greater autonomy is granted . . . by law."

All but one of the central questions connected with this decision to throw the weight and power of the state behind cooperatives can be answered without serious difficulty. Castro was responsible for the action and he has never dodged the issue. He made the decision on the grounds that the cooperatives were appropriate to the gregarious, community-style-of-life which was an existing cultural characteristic of the Cuban peasants and which both they and Castro valued per se; that it facilitated the rapid improvement of rural life in Cuba; that the cooperative system would prevent the re-establishment of a system of large estates by private owners (either Cuban or American); and that it created a more efficient means of diversifying and improving Cuban agriculture.

The action was unquestionably legal by the explicit language and meaning of at least four principal articles of the 1940 Constitution.

The results, if not immediately and overwhelmingly a total success, have certainly been beneficial. Consider, for example, Draper's testimony of 1960 on this point: "No matter what one may think of the theory behind Cuba's land reform program and no matter how the program turns out in practice, there is no getting around the fact that for the poor, illiterate, landless, outcast *guajiros,* the cooperatives represent a jump of centuries in living standards. They also represent a vast increase of constructive activity in the rural areas that were formerly the most backward and stagnant part of Cuba."

Rivero bases his general judgment on a careful review of specific improvements: modern buildings, tile floors, running water, toilets, electricity, free medical and dental care, and similar advantages. He then offers a moving evocation of the spirit of the Revolution that is also a tribute to his own integrity and concern for Cuba: "Castro's revolution is aimed at raising many people out of inhuman squalor and bringing to them some hope of a decent life. In less than three years the Castro Government has accomplished many good things for the underdog. . . . It has tried to improve the living standards of the peasant and the unskilled worker, bringing to them not only welfare benefits but that intangible essential element of prideful participation in the present and hope for the future which is the keynote to the progress and self-respect of the human being. . . . I have seen many of these achievements of the Cuban revolution myself."

Or consider the straightforward judgment of the *Miami Herald* of December 30, 1959: "The common man of Cuba has gained much."

The debatable question involved with the cooperatives concerns whether the stress placed upon them, for which Castro was responsible, involves a betrayal of Castro's pre-victory pledges about agrarian reform. Several aspects of this issue have to be evaluated in making any serious judgment. In the first place, Castro never ducked the responsibility for the decision to emphasize cooperatives and push them with the power of the Revolution and the government. Cubans knew from the beginning that his influence dominated the law.

Next, it should constantly be kept in mind that Castro's government did distribute land to peasants. Rivero's testimony on this point is verified and elaborated by many other observers.

Finally, Castro's remarks about land reform prior to the fall of Batista are open to legitimate differences of interpretation and emphasis. His speeches have never been characterized by the kind of precise, meticulous use of language that one associates with writers like Henry James, politicians like Winston Churchill or Adlai Stevenson, or with the use of mathematical or other scientific symbols. His references to cooperatives have always to be evaluated, furthermore, in the context of his avowed purpose of making a thoroughgoing social revolution designed to change the institutions as well as the structure of existing Cuban society; and of his commitment to the Constitution of 1940, under which cooperatives are certainly legal as a means of discharging the obligations concerning economic development and agrarian diversification which are placed upon the government.

The issue thus involves something considerably less black-and-white than is suggested by the term *betrayal*. Castro stressed cooperatives while making individual grants to peasants. Hence the question can only be answered within this framework: when does a shift in emphasis, that is in line with a fundamental revolutionary outlook, and that is made in response to rapidly changing circumstances, become a betrayal? Clearly enough, it *can* become that kind of an act. But Castro's policy on cooperatives does not, on balance, seem to have involved such a betrayal of his commitment to revolutionary agrarian reform.

This judgment is reinforced by Castro's later willingness, as in May, 1962, to modify the policy after trying it for a period of time. Nor is it very meaningful to talk—as Draper does—about mistakes in estimating a situation, and the opportunities it offers, as though such errors are acts of betrayal. That is to make the classic error of confusing matters of judgment with issues of morality.

In any event, the argument concerning Castro's betrayal of the Revolution by emphasizing cooperatives is considerably less important than the way the Agrarian Reform Law provoked vigorous and overt opposition within and against the revolutionary government. The charge of betrayal became to some extent a rallying cry used by that opposition. Some who employed it, and others who responded to it, undoubtedly did so in perfect sincerity: they thought Castro had turned his back on reform to take up with revolution. Others, and there were many of them, simply used the accusation as a conscious mask or an unconscious rationalization for opposition that was based on defending their special economic, social, and political interests.

This Cuban opposition to the agrarian reform program was reinforced and encouraged by the negative reaction of the United States when the law formally went into effect on June 3, 1959. The combined resistance gravely intensified the existing crisis of the Revolution. Castro sought to meet the challenge in two ways. He used direct armed action against the conservatives and their allies who were trying to overthrow the government. And he made a broad policy decision that represented his second calculated risk: he accepted increasingly general and extensive participating support from the Cuban Communist Party in the revolutionary coalition and government.

This decision ultimately led to action that went far beyond the original willingness to accept the support, and to use the talents, of a small number of individual Communists. That early, and basically ad hoc, relationship between Castro's coalition and Communists finally became, after the counterrevolutionary invasion of 1961, formal collaboration between Castro's 26th July Movement and the Cuban Communist Party. This evolving pattern has generally been misunderstood, over simplified, or distorted. The most widely accepted interpretation holds that Castro was either a Communist from the outset or that he became one some time late in 1959. The evidence simply does not support that argument. At the other extreme, some commentators maintain that Castro's involvement with the Communists dates only from the announcement of their formal collaboration. That thesis is too brittle to explain the reality.

Actually, it may even be somewhat misleading to talk in terms of Castro taking a calculated risk in connection with his relationship to the Communists. Given Castro's temperament, and the rapidly changing character of the Cuban situation, there is some point in arguing that he was not the type, and did not have the opportunity, to sit down and balance out the need for such radical support against the dangers involved in allowing a tightly organized and disciplined Communist Party to extend the activities of its members within the revolutionary government. Such an argument would instead maintain that Castro drifted into a position where he had no choice but to abandon the Revolution or to accept and formalize the Communist Party's participation in the government.

On balance, however, I think that analysis underestimates the extent to which Castro understood what was happening vis-à-vis the Communists beginning in the latter part of the summer of 1959. Increasing numbers of Communists were being appointed to positions in the central and provincial agencies of the revolutionary government. Castro was not ignorant of that development. But it did not mean that the 26th July Movement and the Communists had come to a general agreement on combining forces. That is why I think the most accurate way of describing the situation is to say that Castro took a calculated risk and accepted the more general and increasing participation by members of the Communist Party in the revolutionary government.

It was a calculated risk because Castro understood the dangers involved: he knew it would antagonize his marginal, and even some of his heretofore committed, supporters; and he realized the dangers of pitting his own loosely organized coalition against a tightly integrated party. And it seems to me that the subsequent history of that decision makes it clear that Castro understood that he was undertaking a political battle that involved action, not just along one or two fronts, but along three fronts. He was joining combat, that is to say, against Cuban conservative and moderate opposition, against the United States government, and to control and limit the influence and power of the Cuban Communist Party inside—and over—the revolutionary government. This was not (and is not) politics as usual, or business as usual, and the evolution of the Revolution cannot be understood within that orthodox framework.

The most crucial aspect of the resulting situation is unfortunately the one that Americans have almost completely failed to understand.

By giving up on Castro, and becoming increasingly negative and antagonistic, the United States closed off the one main chance Castro had to make his Revolution without turning to the Communists in Cuba and to the Soviet Union.

Cuban conservatives naturally opposed Castro with increasing fervor as they realized he was not fooling about making a real social revolution. Cuban Communists naturally sought to increase their influence and control over the Revolution. These points are elementary—part of the political facts of life. For that matter, their further meaning is not very difficult to understand if thought is substituted for fear and pride. Given the normal behavior of the conservatives and the Communists, the one way for Castro to keep the support of the moderates— and limit the influence of the Cuban Communists—was for the United States to help him honor his commitment to the Cuban Constitution of 1940 by carrying through a social revolution that would drastically improve the substance and tone of Cuban life.

That is precisely what the United States gave no indication of doing in the summer and early fall of 1959, and Castro was confronted with the situation which led him to take the calculated risk of accepting increasing participation by Cuban Communists in the revolutionary government.

10

The Revolution Embattled at Home and Castro's Second Calculated Risk

The period between the promulgation of the Agrarian Reform Law on May 17 and the sentencing of Major Huber Matos to 20 years imprisonment on charges of treason in December, 1959, was characterized by sustained opposition to the Revolution from various segments of Cuban society. The Agrarian Reform Law extended and increased the disaffection among upper- and middle-class Cubans that had become apparent by the end of February. Some Cubans of the lower-middle and lower classes—urban and rural—supported this opposition in fluctuating numbers and with varying degrees of overt action. In addition, the continuing depression, and the confusion and mistakes incident to implementing the revolutionary program, prompted many people who continued to support Castro to criticize the government within the framework of their underlying sympathy. And finally, Castro's ultimate acceptance of formal support from the Cuban Communist Party increased all such opposition and criticism.

It is essential, however, to realize that the overt anti-Castro opposition began and continued as an attack on the Revolution per se. Men of that counter-revolutionary persuasion worried from the outset about Communist influence in the government as part of their basic antagonism to the radicalism of the Revolution. The Agrarian Reform Law intensified and crystallized such opposition, caused a shake-up in the cabinet, and initiated a series of events which led ultimately to the American planned, financed, and directed invasion of Cuba in 1961.

The dramatic overture to that grand finale was the defection, near the end of June, of Major Pedro Luis Diaz Lanz, head of the Cuban air force. No one has ever given direct, sworn public testimony on whether Diaz Lanz discussed and arranged his defection with American officials while he was still in Cuba. But there are two illuminating bits of evidence which suggest, at the very least, that he quickly established such contacts when he reached the United States—if he had in fact not already made them.

The first is a generally neglected part of the Cuban story as told by former Vice President Richard Nixon in his volume of political memoirs on *Six Crises*. Everyone has noted Nixon's reference to his memorandum of April, 1959, written after his conversation with Castro: the Vice President proposed arming and otherwise supporting an exile force for direct military intervention against Castro and the Revolution. Since it was not acted upon at that time, Nixon's move is de-emphasized save as the initial conception of the final invasion plan. It may have been that, although it seems probable that other American officials were proposing the same kind of policy.

It is usually overlooked, however, that Nixon goes on to note that the Central Intelligence Agency and J. Edgar Hoover, chief of the Federal Bureau of Investigation, agreed with his recommendation. Now Hoover's agency is part of the same Justice Department that also controls the Immigration and Naturalization Service, and he is known upon many occasions to have cooperated with the latter unit. Hoover has also collaborated extensively with the House Committee on Un-American Activities and the Senate Internal Security Subcommittee.

There is considerably more than passing interest, therefore, in the point that it was agents of the Immigration and Naturalization Service who delivered Diaz Lanz to the Senate Internal Security Subcommittee some two weeks after he came ashore in Florida. Encouraged by the friendly welcome offered by Senators James O. Eastland and Thomas J. Dodd of the Committee, Diaz Lanz proceeded to attack Castro, the Cuban government, and the Revolution as being either the dupes, allies, or victims of Communists. The burden of his remarks was that Cuba was well along the road to being a Soviet satellite, and that the United States ought to act promptly and effectively. This description and analysis created a very inaccurate and misleading picture of the Cuban situation. But Senators Dodd and Eastland gave credence to the story by providing Diaz Lanz a public platform and by extending him their sympathy and support. In doing those things they also provided aid, comfort, and quasi-official American support to the counter-revolutionary movement.

Eastland and Dodd seem also to have scored a minor coup within the United States government. Not only were the Cubans taken completely off-guard, but it appears that the White House, the State Department, and even the CIA, were equally surprised and shocked. It may be that Hoover also won a round in his friendly rivalry with Allen Dulles, head of the CIA. Be that as it may, the Dodd-Eastland production created serious consequences within Cuba.

Castro dismissed the protestations of innocence by the Eisenhower administration and interpreted the whole affair as direct American intervention in the affairs of the Revolution. It provoked from him the first unequivocally hostile speech since the fall of Batista. It is no answer to say that Castro and other Cubans should have known that Eastland and Dodd did not have formal authority over foreign policy. They undoubtedly knew that. They were also aware that the Congress does exert considerable direct and indirect influence on the President and the Secretary of State.

This routine constitutional and political authority of the Congress in foreign affairs had been increased by Senator Joseph McCarthy. His technique was a model of classic simplicity: he simply used the ideology of the Cold War against the very people who formulated the ideology. Beginning in 1945, President Harry S. Truman had blamed all the troubles of the world on the Soviet Union and its Communist allies. Liberals and conservatives had accepted that analysis. McCarthy merely projected the assumptions of that anti-Communist outlook to their logical conclusions and then acted upon them.

McCarthy was dead in 1959, but the technique and its effectiveness were in excellent health. Along with many other foreign leaders, Castro and his government colleagues also realized that the practice of McCarthyism had become institutionalized. For all these reasons, they were quite intelligently upset and concerned about the Diaz Lanz episode. They understood that Dodd and Eastland were using the testimony of Diaz Lanz to stereotype the Cuban Revolution and fit it into the crude good guy-bad guy plot of the Cold War which was so widely accepted in 1959.

Given this background, Castro's reaction is not very difficult to fathom. Already confronted by internal opposition to the land reform, and by increasing Communist activity in Cuba, he saw the Dodd-Eastland performance as a move by the United States, or at the very least an important segment of the policymaking community, to support that resistance by labeling the revolution Communist and thus invoking all the antagonistic emotions and fears associated with the Soviet Union. This reaction was reinforced by Castro's persistent concern about the upper non-commissioned ranks and the officer corps of Batista's old army. It was in connection with a group of former air force officers, for example, that Castro had insisted upon a second trial during the early weeks of the Revolution—a retrial for which he provided a directed verdict of guilty.

Castro had not by July, 1959, made any moves toward accepting general, extensive participating support from the Cuban Communist Party in the revolutionary government. His appointment of individual Communists was something fundamentally different—risky, perhaps, but different—and the two things should not be equated. For just that reason, the Eastland-Dodd attack angered Castro and reinforced his fears of American support for the anti-revolutionary forces. His temperament and earlier behavior also suggests that he was determined—perhaps personally so even more than ideologically —not to be forced into the position of proving his non-Communist credentials at the call and to the satisfaction of two American Senators. Particularly since their reputation for honoring the first rules of evidence was less than impressive. It seems very likely, moreover, that the affair intensified Castro's feelings that he needed all the aid he could muster in support of the Revolution.

Castro seemed, indeed, almost to panic. Perhaps he did. Castro is, after all, a human being. He was (and is) a very young man in a position of grave responsibility. And he was (and is) an emotional man deeply committed to a radical revolution. Finally, he was (and is) in a very tight spot—a radical revolutionary operating 90 miles from the most powerful nation in the world whose policy takes the form of a dedicated and relatively unsophisticated anti-Communism.

Such an interpretation is reinforced by his action in the situation created when Cuban President Manuel Urrutia Lleo responded to the Diaz Lanz defection by attacking the former Major as a traitor, but also going on to warn against Communist influence in Cuba. Now Urrutia was neither a notably competent leader nor an ardent advocate of the revolutionary program; but he was the one judge of the Urgency Court who had stood out against Batista's proceedings against some of Castro's early supporters. His position in the Cuban government was openly known to be the result of Castro's respect and affection for that earlier performance.

But Castro launched a savage attack on Urrutia in response to the President's speech, and then resigned as premier to force him out of the government. It was a grossly exaggerated display of power, ruthless far beyond the need of the situation. It may be, of course, that Castro knew even then (mid-July) of the major conspiracy being organized against the Revolution. If that was the case, then his action can in part be explained and understood as a demonstration intended to warn and cow as many of those opponents as possible. Even so, the feeling persists that Castro stood shaking in the doorway to panic.

Yet he turned back, and on August 7, 1959, restored the rights of habeas corpus which had been periodically suspended since the early days of the Revolution. That move was indicative of Castro's fundamental outlook, and also suggests that he had recovered his nerve. That, in turn, may have been prompted by a confidence that was soon justified. On August 11, the government began an almost wholly successful move against a serious conspiracy involving wealthy landowners, former members of Batista's army, and other Cubans who were either purposively opposed to the Agrarian Reform and other features of the Revolution, or who had been persuaded—or hired— to join the movement. The counter-revolutionary effort was broken up in a series of direct military operations which included one highly dramatic and effective bit of counter-espionage leading to the entrapment of a plane bringing men and supplies to the conspiracy.

Castro still faced three grave problems. The first was the continuing and increasing pressure on the Revolution exerted by the depression. Castro had to have economic assistance of some kind, and fast, if he was to finance the revolutionary program and at the same time maintain a tolerable level of economic well-being in the country. To keep the image favored by American policy-makers, Castro was nosing into the wringer and he knew it.

He also knew that the United States was not going to help him—or the Cuban people—avoid that torment. Castro's protest of March 23 against the counter-revolutionary activities of exiles based in Florida had been deftly deflected by Washington, and the harassment had continued. It may be that J. Edgar Hoover's sympathy with Nixon's memorandum in favor of supporting the anti-Castro groups contributed to the inefficiency of the FBI in coping with the exiles. Or it may simply have resulted from indifference. But the United States could have stopped the activity had it cared enough to do so. It did not. Americans have never undergone such harassment, and they are very prone to discount its effect. They might establish some empathy with the situation, however, by making a serious effort to imagine their own reactions if random propaganda and bombing raids were undertaken and sustained against their state and local governments, and against the primary economic activities of their area.

Washington made a considerably more impressive showing against the Agrarian Reform Law than it did against the Cuban exiles. The United States government note of June 11, 1959, was proper, cold, blunt, and more than a bit intimidating. It did acknowledge Cuba's right under international law to take American property. It neglected to mention that the action was not only legal, but also and explicitly a directed responsibility, under the Cuban Constitution of 1940. State Department officials instead developed their argument along a different line. Cuba was advised that such expropriation was legal only with the fulfillment of "the corresponding obligation on the part of a state that such taking will be accompanied by payment of prompt, adequate, and effective compensation."

This is impressive, even slightly awesome, language. The facts and the law in support thereof are considerably less so. Only part of this American formula has any accepted standing in international jurisprudence.[1] That concerns the basic obligation to pay compensation. The additional American demand that it be "prompt, adequate, and effective" is wholly American in origin and standing. Both the injunction and phrase itself came from Secretary of State Hull as one of his contributions to the Good Neighbor policy. He produced it as part of

---

1. See the excellent new study by A. A. Fatouros, *Government Guarantees to Foreign Investors* (New York, Columbia University Press, 1962), and the items in his fine bibliography.

his campaign to intimidate and coerce Mexico during the oil controversy.

The point is that no poor or developing country has the funds for "prompt, adequate, and effective compensation." Such governments are nationalizing foreign property in order to accumulate both the psychological and the economic capital they cannot obtain in any other way. They need a sense of ownership as well as the productive property per se to sustain the process of development.

Hence the American demand is relevant only as a vehicle for the implied threat that the United States will resort to other means if its formal injunction is not honored. This meaning was only slightly veiled in the note to Cuba. The United States made it clear that it would "seek solutions through other appropriate international procedures" if Cuba did not meet the American conditions.

And as Castro knew, his offer to pay compensation in 20-year bonds at about four percent interest, with the amount to be based on the evaluation provided by the American firms for Cuban tax purposes, was not satisfactory to the United States government. It *was* reasonable, but the United States had refused to consider a very similar offer in connection with the expropriation of United Fruit Company land in Guatemala. That comparison raised still another unhappy thought. The Cubans undoubtedly recalled, when they read the American note, that the United States in dealing with Guatemala had included counter-revolutionary coups financed, planned, and directed by the CIA as part of "other appropriate international procedures."

The American note carried still another, and even more direct, kind of intimidating reference. American opposition to the Agrarian Reform Law was linked specifically to "matters of deep and legitimate interest to the United States consumers of Cuban products," as well as to "investors in Cuba." It must be granted that there was a somewhat unusual kind of subtlety in the way the State Department couched this threat in terms of concern for the "consumers." The housewife as an instrument of the national interest—and of those of the corporation—offers an image sufficiently incongruous as to be almost charming in its effect. But one should not miss the gaff inside the gingham. Certainly the Cubans did not. The Department of State was clearly raising the possibility that Cuba would lose its sugar quota in the American market if it did not pay "prompt, adequate, and effective compensation"—or if it did not back down on the expropriation of American property.

It went on, furthermore, to pose the same kind of threat in connection with "private and public investment." Not only was the State Department telling Castro that it would discourage private investors, but—and even more importantly—it was formally warning him that he was losing any slight remaining chance for a public (or government) loan from any agency in which the United States exerted its mighty influence. Against this background of multiple threats, the United States suggested that Castro might reconsider his action, giving "considerate treatment" to the opinions as well as the property of American investors.

The American note of June 11, 1959, was thus deceptively short and formal. It was in many ways a bit of a masterpiece in its own peculiar idiom: facile, tough, and intimidating. It gave obvious support and meaning to the continuing demands in the Congress for using the sugar quota to discipline Castro and mute his Revolution. Coupled with the Diaz Lanz episode, the American stand on the Agrarian Reform Law greatly increased the tension and prompted two perceptive and responsible American observers to call for immediate action to prevent the situation from deteriorating beyond recall. Walter Lippmann warned the United States in July of the grave danger inherent in its basic posture toward the Cuban Revolution: "The thing we should never do in dealing with revolutionary countries, in which the world abounds, is to push them behind an iron curtain raised by ourselves." And aware not only that this was happening, but also of the crucial role of the Cuban depression in the entire situation, Roscoe Drummond called for positive action. He proposed that Undersecretary of State Dillon proceed immediately to Havana with a direct offer of aid in order to stabilize the economic crisis. That would break the dynamic pattern that was becoming so threatening, allow everyone involved to relax, and create an atmosphere more favorable to a compromise settlement of other issues.

Drummond's extremely acute and responsible suggestion was not acted upon. The policy of the United States remained one of letting Castro and the Cubans go through the wringer. Along with a good many Congressmen, Senator Olin D. Johnson of South Carolina wanted the process speeded up. To Johnson and his supporters, at any rate, it was a simple matter of equity. "Any nation which is receiving so much from another nation as Cuba is from the United States, should be less hostile and more friendly to us. Certainly we are in a position to bargain our sugar markets with Cuba for more cooperation."

In line with this outlook, Johnson and Senator Styles Bridges (who also favored disciplining Castro) introduced an anti-Castro amendment to the Mutual Security Act of 1959. It stipulated that no aid could be extended to a country expropriating American property until a satisfactory settlement had been made. Remarking bluntly that the action was motivated by a desire to hurt Castro, Senator Fulbright went on to suggest that the moral and pragmatic issues were a bit more complicated.

Fulbright relied on a bit of common sense psychology to make his point: "When a big country such as ours begins to threaten a small country like Cuba . . . it probably [has] the opposite reaction to that intended." We might learn a bit of that lesson, he added in a pointed effort to jar Johnson into some awareness of the issues, by observing the way southerners responded to a similar kind of tough talk from northerners in connection with the Negro problem. Fulbright was ignored. The amendment passed. And instead of halting such threats, or leading to changes in American policy, Fulbright's warning turned out to be an unhappily accurate prophecy.

Castro's success in breaking up the counter-revolutionary movement headed by landowners and former army personnel did not ease the pressure exerted on the Revolution by the economic crisis and by American policy. Those factors, coupled with the radical nature of the Revolution and Castro's determination to sustain its momentum, prompted continuing criticism and opposition from moderates within and outside the government. Castro's call of August 27, 1959, for a closing of ranks to strengthen and sustain the Revolution indicated his awareness of this ferment as well as his public recognition that the Revolution was in trouble. "The hour has arrived," he exhorted, "to fight and work for the triumph of the country, since we must all triumph or we will all go down together."

There is considerable evidence that Castro made another effort, during late July and August, to obtain economic assistance from the United States. This probably involved approaches to private bankers as well as to the government and the International Monetary Fund. Representative Daniel Flood, for example, referred to negotiations for a $300 million loan and warned against granting such help. Another *New York Times* story by E. W. Kenworthy (from Washington on August 9) also indicated that some kind of discussions had been going on. Changing the metaphor a bit, American officials told Kenworthy that the Cuban economic crisis had Castro "in a box." They again admitted that a loan would ease the crisis. But as Kenworthy reported, the terms had not changed. "The United States would make such a loan only if the Castro regime agreed to the kind of stabilization program that the International Monetary Fund has worked out with other nations in similar trouble." Kenworthy's story probably chronicled the end of the talks.

In any event, Cuba announced three days later, on August 12, that it was selling 170,000 tons of sugar to the Soviet Union. The transaction was praised by Pazos, still head of the National Bank of Cuba: "The effects of this sale on the market will be highly constructive." This deal (and the one for 330,000 tons at the end of September) have often been interpreted as being so unusual as to signify Castro's commitment to the Communist bloc.

This is an erroneous interpretation on at least two counts. First of all, it was not a unique operation. Sugar sales to Russia were a routine part of Cuba's effort to market the portion of its crop which was not taken by the United States. The tonnage figures for the previous four years under Batista were: 442,915 in 1955, 206,361 in 1956, 347,673 in 1957, and 182,148 in 1958. Secondly, Castro did not become a satellite through the sales in 1959, nor was he trying to do so in making them. As in the earlier years, Cuba sold sugar any place it could find a market—and had often closed such deals at a price below the international figure. Actually, Pazos was far too optimistic in his estimate of the deal. It of course helped Cuba, but it did not begin to meet the economic crisis. That continued.

So did American opposition. Despite what was reported on September 4 from Havana as "a very cordial meeting" between Ambassador Bonsal and Castro, the United States nevertheless recalled Bonsal for talks in Washington that same day. A report from Washington verified the implication that the move was connected with American pressure on the Revolution. Government officials acknowledged that Bonsal was called home to "underscore the United States' displeasure," and added that the talks would involve "more than routine consultations."

First verification of this came later in the month when the United States ignored Cuba's call in the United Nations for action on Castro's plan for a $30-billion developmental loan to Latin America. A similar indicator was provided by the lackadaisical response to Cuba's protest on October 8 against counter-revolutionary preparations in the United States. Cuba continued to suffer raids and harassment from planes based in America. Near the end of the month, furthermore, a counter-revolutionary organization named the White Rose (and headed by Castro's former brother-in-law) formally announced its operations.

Midway through the month, on October 14, the main purpose of Bonsal's return to Washington became fully apparent. It had indeed been a visit for "more than routine consultations." The United States fired off a second note opposing the ex-propriation and other provisions of the Agrarian Reform Law. While still cool, this second note was considerably stronger. It was far less subtle in making the point that economic sanctions would be used if Cuba did not accede to American specifications on the speed, form, and amount of compensation to be paid American citizens. "If Fidel Castro takes time out to read the note," the *Chicago Daily News* commented, "he will get the clear implication that Cuba will get rough treatment from Congress next year unless it begins some serious talks with the State Department on the problems of American sugar and other properties in Cuba."

Such was the general and specific situation when Major Huber Matos, a revolutionary leader who had joined Castro in March, 1958, used his position to increase the domestic pressure on the government. Because the episode is an important one, and because Draper and other commentators have interpreted it in extreme terms, it seems useful to examine the matter with some care.[1] Originally a school teacher, Matos became active in the opposition to Batista at a relatively early

---

1. Draper hangs much of his interpretation of the Revolution on the Matos affair. The most straightforward account calling attention to aspects neglected by Draper is by Herbert L. Matthews, *The Cuban Story* (New York, Braziller, 1961).

date. He was a capable, hard-working resistance man who fought through to the victory over Batista, becoming in the process a key figure holding the highest military rank in the army of Camagüey Province. While he was not a member of the original 26th of July Movement, and had never revealed himself as a militant social revolutionary, Matos was a man who had earned his position of power and authority inside the government, and his general popularity in the province. The school teacher become major in the revolutionary army was an honorable, serious, and responsible figure.

From an early date, certainly by the summer of 1959, Matos had come to question and oppose at least two Castro policies. He criticized the appointment of individual Cuban Communists to positions in the government before Castro began to accept the increasingly general participating support of Communists, and he fought the latter development as it evolved. At the same time, Matos resisted the tempo—and very probably the extent—of the radical changes being pushed through by the Castro government. In particular, he used his power and authority to slow down the application of the Agrarian Reform Law to the cattle industry in Camagüey Province.

Matos sought, over a period of time, to raise at least the Communist issue with Castro. He grew increasingly disturbed as more Communists were appointed to positions of military as well as civilian influence and power in Camagüey. He was never granted an audience with Castro. Matos did, however, make his views well known in the province, and particularly to his officer corps. He carried on an uninhibited educational program based on his own views. He was a political officer, and the politics were his. In these important respects, Matos enjoyed and exercised great freedom.

Matos submitted his resignation on October 19, four days after the tough American note on the Agrarian Reform Law, and in the midst of a flurry of air raids staged by exiles based in the United States. But Matos did not simply resign. He could have done that, and returned to teaching school, without doing any of the other things connected with his action. Actually, it is more than a little condescending—as well as inaccurate —to treat Matos as an innocent or naïve young scholar who wanted to get out of politics.

Matos was resigning and taking with him a nucleus of trained military officers and experienced political leaders. Let Draper describe the group: "a majority of the Camagüey army leaders, the head of the 26th of July Movement in the province, and others resigned with him."

Castro moved immediately. He arrested Matos on October 20 and charged him with treason. By the definition provided in the Constitution of the United States,[1] a standard almost impossible to improve upon, Matos had not committed treason. But neither was his action the modest little performance that Draper seems to imply. Matos had not committed an overt act against the regime. But he had personally persuaded a significant number of important men under his military and political command to leave government service.

Castro's charge of treason was based on the argument that Matos had thereby abused and exceeded his official responsibility in a way that threatened an already embattled revolutionary government. Castro also attacked the reasons Matos gave for his action. He denied that either the Revolution or the government was Communist. "Ours is not a Communist revolution. Ours is, I admit, a radical revolution—probably the most radical in Cuban history." And in his testimony at the Matos trial, Raúl Castro said flatly that "we will fight the Communists" if they "place themselves against the Revolution."

Several important considerations must be kept in mind when evaluating the Matos episode. First, the Revolution was in a serious crisis. Second, the American definition of treason

1. "Treason against the United States, shall consist only in levying War against them, or in adhering to their Enemies, giving them Aid and Comfort."

does not hold in Cuba—or most other countries, for that matter. The far more common definition of treason hinges upon action considered inimical to the existing state. Even Draper concedes that possibility—"so it might have been"—in connection with the action by Matos. Third, Castro did *not* proceed in the same fashion against six important cabinet members who left the government over the Communist issue on November 26, more than a month after Matos was arrested. Here is a crucial difference in treatment that offers an important insight into the Matos episode. Castro's quick crackdown on Matos is explained by the Major's significantly more dangerous kind of action.

The American definition of treason is relevant to the Matos affair only in the sense that it provides a basis on which to say that it would be better, or more desirable, if every country—and Cuba in particular—adopted and honored the definition of treason in the Constitution of the United States. Even if this were the case, however, Castro's action against Matos would hardly become unique. It is not necessary to charge a man with treason under the treason article in the American Constitution in order to sentence him to 20 years' imprisonment for conduct considered dangerous to the state.

This very point was made in rather telling fashion by Congressman Walter Judd during a discussion of the early revolutionary proceedings against Batista's associates. "No government in power, whether legitimate or otherwise," Judd patiently reminded his fellow Congressmen, "is likely to continue full constitutional rights and privileges if those privileges are taken advantage of to increase the disorder and the efforts to overthrow the government."

Castro took the resignations of Matos and his supporters as representing a clear and present danger to the Revolution as well as to the revolutionary government. He followed the arrest of Matos by again revoking habeas corpus (at the end of October), by making (in November) a four percent assessment on the wages of workers to help accumulate capital for industrialization, and by intervening (also in November) to sustain Communist Party influence and participation in the ruling body of the Cuban Confederation of Labor.

This was Castro's crucial move in his calculated tactical risk of accepting general and increasing Communist Party participation in the revolutionary government. He said he took the step in the need as well as the name of unity, and that was clearly part of his motivation. He felt the Revolution was entering a time of troubles and that it needed all the *radical* support it could muster. As this suggests, Castro's move was largely a negative act. To be sure, Castro's neo-populist outlook certainly led him toward Marxism once the circumstances confronting the Revolution became so difficult and threatening. So, too, did the intellectual and emotional Marxism of close associates like his brother Raúl and Guevara. But Castro was not a Communist then, and it seems very improbable that he has become one since.

Whatever the combination of reasons that drove and encouraged Castro to accept organized Communist Party participation in the government, he did so on the central—and perhaps arrogant—assumption that he and the July 26th Movement could always control or defeat the Communists on crucial substantive issues and in the fundamental matters of running the Revolution and the country.

It is thus confusing and misleading to talk, as Draper does, about "old" and "new" Communists in connection with Castro's decision. Draper's old Communists are Communists: the pre-1959 leaders and members of the Cuban Communist Party. But the men and women he calls new Communists are in fact non-Communist Cuban radicals who have undertaken the extremely difficult, risky, and demanding job of using the Communist Party to effect their own revolutionary purposes. Draper is by no means the most perceptive guide to what happened in Cuba during the last half of 1959. Neither is there

137

much help to be found in the writings of Karl Marx, or in the histories of the Russian and the Chinese revolutions.

The single most insightful remark about this phase of the Cuban Revolution was made by F. Scott Fitzgerald at the end of the 1920's. Aware of all the many major reforms that the United States needed, and deeply discouraged by the lack of any militant, non-Communist radical political force either prepared or equipped to undertake them, Fitzgerald offered an aphorism as a possible guide to action: "It may be necessary to join the Communist Party in order to have the revolution."

That is the only sense in which Castro and his radical supporters joined the Cuban Communist Party. Castro accepted general Communist participation in the government, and the Party's organizational framework, as a means to sustain his own 26th of July Revolution. He has made compromises, some of them very serious and portentous ones, and he has discovered that it is impossible to maintain full control of the situation at all times. He has also resorted to harsh measures against political opposition, and to severe economic measures which have lowered the standard of living to which some—but by no means all— Cubans were accustomed in the years immediately before the Revolution.

But Castro has never, either in 1959 or in 1962, given or surrendered his Revolution to the Communist Party in Cuba. He has always fought the Party on key issues. He is still doing so today. But he has never been given any understanding or sympathy—let alone encouragement or help—either by critics such as Draper or by the United States government.

11

The Revolution Assaulted from Abroad

The United States quickly interpreted Castro's actions of late 1959, and his trade deal with the Soviet Union early in 1960, as meaning that Cuba had become a totalitarian Communist satellite. Most commentators have followed that official government line. Neither claim is factually correct. But the ideology which provided that simple, arbitrary explanation of a very complex reality is nevertheless important because it also produced the counter-revolutionary invasion of Cuba in April, 1961, almost 63 years to the day after the United States went to war to pacify Cuba in 1898.

It appears very probable, indeed, that the CIA began before the end of 1959 to work with counter-revolutionary groups in Cuba. This activity increased throughout 1960 and into the first months of 1961. Along the way, it involved active American military support in providing air cover for the smuggling of arms and other supplies to Castro's enemies in Cuba. The formal American decision to arm and train an exile army, however, was not made until March, 1960.

This chronology of its Cuban operations, along with a great deal of other evidence, makes it perfectly clear that it is the CIA—rather than the military—which functions as an independent variable in the formulation and conduct of American foreign policy. The military does have great influence, both directly within the government and indirectly through its ties with the industrial complex of the country. Civilians gave the military such influence by defining the world in military terms (both in 1939 and again in 1945), but the military cannot independently conceive and mount an operation having immediate and profound effects on foreign policy.

139

The CIA not only *can* do that, it *has done* it a good many times. The CIA has originated projects, persuaded the President and other high officials to authorize them on the basis of information provided by the CIA, and then executed the operation through its own agents. It is a self-validating civilian agency with vast areas of independent action in foreign policy. And it was created and is sustained by civilians.

The real points at issue in all this do not concern the wearing of uniforms after being graduated and commissioned from one of the service academies. The questions involve the far more important matters of how one explains America's difficulties and defines its opportunities, and whether or not one is willing to resort to force in solving the problems or exploiting the openings. These subjects are crucial to an understanding of the invasion of Cuba.

The American propensity to externalize evil is at least as well developed as any known to history. We have followed that self-righteous path of least resistance since we won our independence. It is wholly unnecessary to dwell either on the extent or the intensity of the manner in which American leaders and the public at large have done this with reference to the Soviet Union. What is not so generally recognized, however, is the degree to which Americans have also externalized good. The extent, that is, to which they have argued (and finally assumed) that America's political and economic well-being are determined by opportunities that exist outside the United States. This began at least as early as Jefferson's reliance on the frontier to underwrite prosperity and representative government, and has continued to the present day. Americans have always relied on a new frontier.

The United States has furthermore exhibited a pronounced tendency to deal with its difficulties, and to exploit its opportunities, through the use (or the threat) of economic or political force. A rudimentary listing of our wars, quasi-wars, police actions, and interventions makes the point. We have fought, in rough order (and counting only the first conflicts since there are several repeaters), the following nations: various Indian tribes that *we* defined as independent societies, England, France, Spain, Canada, Mexico, Nicaragua, Hawaii, China, Colombia, Germany, Austria-Hungary, various other Latin American governments, Japan, Italy, several Eastern European countries, Koreans, and sundry other Asians. We have applied strong—even massive—economic force as a conscious instrument of policy to every nation with which we have ever had significant relations. None of this makes us unique. Other major powers have their own lists. But that is just the point. We are not unique.

These features of American thought and action in foreign affairs have characterized the policy of the United States toward Cuba not only since 1895, but in particular since Senator Morse's warning to the Cubans on January 12, 1959. By the end of that year, the two official notes on the Agrarian Reform Law (along with many others concerning American property rights), and the increasing agitation to discipline Castro (evil) and thereby re-open Cuba to American influence (good), made it clear that the traditional outlook was as dominant as ever.

On November 29, 1959, for example, Senator Ellender fired another volley on the sugar quota issue. A bit later, on December 10, Secretary of State Christian Herter made it known that Castro's offer on compensation for American property was no more acceptable than the earlier and similar Guatemalan proposal. And as the Congress reconvened in January, 1960, a consensus began to emerge very rapidly around the idea, as one Representative put it, that "this is a time for action and not pussy-footing."

The outcry that greeted Cuba's barter deal with the Russians in February, 1960, could have been predicted. This bargain was largely the result of three factors. First, Castro's serious economic problems. Second, America's refusal to help solve those difficulties save in a way that would subvert the Revolution. And third, the not particularly astute realization by the Soviets that they could exploit those two conditions in a way that might bring them significant gains. American policy—long-run and short term—handed the Russians an opening which they promptly exploited. The United States had both the power and the opportunity to avoid that situation. It did not do so.

The greatest gain that Russia ultimately won from its decision to aid Castro concerned the opportunity it finally secured to sit in on the game that the United States had been playing ever since 1945. Moscow could at last talk about its ally on the border of the United States. And it unquestionably began to use Cuba, as it already used other Latin American countries, as a center for the distribution of propaganda and as a base for intelligence operations.

But there was in 1960, and as of September, 1962, there still is, a vital difference. The Russians did not establish Soviet bases in Cuba as the United States has done in such nations as Turkey along the frontiers of the Soviet Union. Moscow constructed no airfields to handle Red Air Force bombers armed with nuclear weapons, built no launching pads for Soviet missiles tipped with hydrogen warheads, and flew no U-2 flights over the United States from Cuba.

The Russians were quite aware of this difference: they understand, even though many Americans seem not to, that their link with Cuba has not changed the essential balance of power which stands in favor of the United States.

American reaction to the Castro-Soviet trade agreement, and to the subsequent development of the tie between the two countries, seems to have been based on the same assumption that produced the policy of containment vis-à-vis the Soviet Union—only this time applied to the United States instead of Russia. It appears to have been grounded, that is, on the axiom that the United States could not continue to exist as a democratic and prosperous capitalist nation if any major European power challenged or blocked or decreased its existing power in, or its potential expansion into, areas and countries along its frontiers.

In any event, President Eisenhower's first response was to approve the proposal to arm and train Cuban counter-revolutionaries. The United States next refused to sell helicopters to Castro. Then, on April 20, 1960, the House of Representatives passed a law prohibiting aid to Castro unless a special finding was made to define and authorize such assistance as being in the interests of the United States. The Cubans seem to have interpreted this last act for what it was—the beginning of the shift from letting Castro "go through the wringer" to a policy of speeding up the process. In any event, the revolutionary government made overtures in May to discuss the deteriorating situation.

The United States declined the offer. Instead, on May 26, 1960, it cancelled all aid programs then in operation. This assistance did not amount to very much, but the move indicated how rapidly America was moving to increase its pressure on Castro. Exactly a month later, the House Committee on Agriculture granted the President power to fix the Cuban sugar quota.

After that act, if not indeed from February, the record of American-Cuban relations reads like the script for a crude burlesque on the action-reaction, vicious-circle kind of diplomacy. Castro next seized the Texaco and Esso refineries for refusing to process Soviet crude petroleum. The American note of protest was strong, inaccurate, rather emotional, and filled with portents of retaliation.

That came from both sides on July 6, 1960. Cuba announced Revolutionary Law 851, which established the legal basis for the general nationalization of American and Cuban property. Seizures under the law began almost immediately and continued throughout the year. For its part, the United States reduced the Cuban sugar quota by 700,000 short tons. A bit later, on July 16, it filed "a most solemn and serious protest" against Law 851. It asserted, contrary to the careful opinion of Cuba's best lawyers (given in response to the inquiries of American business interests), that the legislation was "manifestly in violation" of international law.[1] The State Department argument was in essence the same one that had been used in connection with the Agrarian Reform Law. Cuba's action was illegal because it failed "to assure the payment of prompt, adequate, and effective compensation." Despite the grave tone of the American note, Cuba did not rescind the law.

Similar rounds of tit-for-tat continued throughout the summer. And the reality of such clashes was to some extent infused with the kind of mounting anger and small-boy behavior generally associated with the game. The specific timing and tone of some of the exchanges, for example, were undoubtedly guided by that spirit of dare and double-dare. But it is a mistake to *explain* the diplomacy in those terms. Each side had embarked upon a broad course of action which generated fundamental opposition from the other, and the details, timing, and tone of the incidents were secondary and derivative in nature.

It is at this point—*but not before*—that Meyer and Szulc offer considerable insight in speaking of the tragic nature of American-Cuban relations. Tragedy is defined by the confrontation and clash of opposing truths. And there was truth on both sides. Cuba's truth involved the need for a thoroughgoing social revolution, the right to carry it through, and the legitimate expectation that its former overlord would either help ease the transition or leave it alone to proceed as it could and would on its own. The American truth involved past concern and assistance, existing rights and economic stakes in Cuba per se,

---

1. See R.C. Allison, "Cuba's Seizure of American Business," *American Bar Association Journal,* 47:1 and 2 (January, February, 1961), 48-51, 187-191.

and the legitimate expectation that the Revolution would make its transition with consideration for those American equities.

There is, as Meyer and Szulc explain, the element of inevitability inherent in the concept of tragedy. The conflict between such clashing truths will produce disaster if neither of the protagonists breaks into and changes the logic of the confrontation. But Meyer and Szulc are mistaken on two important counts. The element of inevitability which they stress is always conditional until *after* the tragedy materializes. *The concept of tragedy is a means of explaining something that has happened.* It does not account for the actual events save in and to the degree that the actors entertain and act upon a tragic outlook. And neither Castro nor American policy-makers were men of that nature. The inevitability that Meyer and Szulc emphasize was *not* present from the outset.

But if we accept the broad conceptual approach of thinking about American-Cuban relations within the framework of tragedy—but abandon the theme of inevitability—then we are able to see and raise the central questions. These concern which protagonist had the greater responsibility for acting to change the tragic logic, and what men made the effort.

The United States had the vastly greater responsibility. It took control of Cuban affairs in the period between 1895 and 1902 and never relinquished its final authority. In addition, it asserted and preened itself on a morality which required it to use that power in ways that would have avoided the conditions of the Cuban political economy in 1958, and which would have led to a different approach to the Revolution of 1959 once it had occurred. By its own actions and its proclaimed morality, therefore, the burden was on the United States.

American policy did not measure up to those responsibilities between 1895 and 1959, or between January, 1959, and the opening of the presidential election campaign in August, 1960. It is conceivable that, without the added pressure and competitive bidding inherent in such a campaign, relations between the United States and Cuba would have continued to be critically difficult without culminating in an invasion. Not only conceivable, but actually rather probable. Formal relations might even have been broken, for example, without leading to such an attack. That kind of temporary hiatus had developed a good many times in the history of American foreign relations.

There are two general reasons for questioning the assumption (or the argument) that things would have worked out as they did even had there been no election campaign. The first of these involves a negative consideration. It may very seriously be doubted that President Eisenhower would ever have given the go-ahead signal for the invasion of Cuba. It is true that he authorized the organization and training of an exile force. But he did so very reluctantly, and that action did not commit him to an invasion.

The decision to launch such an assault would have cut across several of Eisenhower's most central character traits. Behind the militant, extremist, and self-righteous rhetoric of Secretary of State Dulles, which attracted most of the attention and comment, stood Eisenhower's far calmer temperament and his deep disinclination to involve the United States in action that violated what he considered to be America's moral integrity.[1] He was a man more concerned with the way power was used than either with its use or merely retaining it.

Eisenhower's stand against the British-French-Israeli invasion of Egypt is a typical example of this central feature of his outlook. He also had a deep aversion to becoming involved in combat operations that cost American lives. This is perhaps the most telling point of all. Let us assume that Eisenhower had come to the point of considering such an invasion of Cuba.

---

1. What many people took to be Eisenhower's "massive inaction" was often just the superficial side of a line of policy based on understanding that apparent passivity often involves action of a very vigorous and far-reaching kind. On Eisenhower and Dulles, see Sherman Adams, *Firsthand Report* (New York, Harper and Bros., 1961).

Let us even assume that he had overcome his moral scruples against violating American law and the obligations of the United States involved in the treaty structure of the Organization of American States. Given those conditions, Eisenhower most assuredly—as a military officer with long experience in such command decisions—would never have considered allowing the operation to fail for want of overt American military action. But that very military realism would have collided with his deep reluctance to send Americans into another battle—and it seems very likely that the latter element would have triumphed.

The second negative factor involved in evaluating the role of the election campaign derives from Eisenhower's unhappy experience with the CIA. Despite his own recurrent doubts, and uneasiness, he went along for four years with that organization's assurances concerning the U-2 flights over the Soviet Union. Then, in a dramatic and never-to-be-forgotten failure, the program destroyed his last chance of achieving his most treasured goal—the working out of an understanding with Russia that would open the way for lasting peace. It may therefore seriously be doubted that he would have relied upon the CIA in another major decision—particularly in view of his own temperament and values.

The positive factor related to questioning the inevitability of the invasion arises out of the role of American-Cuban relations in the election campaign, and from the essential character and outlook of the two candidates—and more particularly of the man who won. It seems probable that Richard Nixon would also have gone ahead with an invasion. After all, he had proposed training the exiles as early as April, 1959. And we now know that his seemingly fundamental attack on John F. Kennedy's Cuban policy during the campaign was a massive deception of the American people undertaken to preserve the pseudo-secrecy of the exile training program. It could be argued, of course, that Nixon would have cut free of the exiles once they were trained and ready. That seems very doubtful, if only because the dynamics of the campaign would have made it very difficult to risk the failure inherent in a policy of real laissez faire. And Eisenhower's influence would have been undercut by Nixon's need to be his own president—as well as by the not-so-latent tension between the two men.

One could make a strong, if never conclusive, argument that the issue of relations with Cuba was one of the two or three crucial elements in the campaign of 1960. A review of all the speeches and random remarks of the candidates reveals a large number of references to the problem, and the question became ever more prominent as the campaign developed. Whatever part it did play in his election, one thing is certain: Kennedy raised and pushed the issue. The responsibility is his.

As in general, so with the Cuban problem: Kennedy's two most central personal characteristics are his urge to power and his fear of failure. He obviously wants power very urgently, and conceives of it in the strikingly narrow terms of himself and his clan. His propensity to personalize substantive issues, as he did in connection with the rise in steel prices in 1962, is unusual even for a man clearly trying to telescope generations into half-decades. His candid definition of prestige, offered during the campaign in connection with foreign public opinion of the United States, is very revealing in this respect. "I define prestige as influence, as an ability to persuade people to accept your point of view." Not just esteem and respect, but power over other people.

Kennedy's concept of power in terms of the clan involves one of the earliest, indeed one of the most primeval, forms of externalizing evil known in human affairs. It is one of the most rudimentary and intense forms of that phenomenon. This underlying propensity to externalize evil converged in Kennedy with another characteristic of clan society—the fear of failure. Those aspects of his outlook reinforced each other, and as they did so they produced in Kennedy an extremely intense concern that time was running out and that control of the future was about to be lost at any moment.

Finally, Kennedy's concept of a New Frontier was very revealing of his outlook even though in reality it was anything but new. He did enumerate various domestic social welfare issues and scientific problems that needed attention, but his underlying theme was the absolute necessity of continued expansion for the American economic system. This did not involve in Kennedy's mind any idea or program of colonial or territorial expansion. It did involve, however, the same kind of overseas economic expansion that had characterized the thinking of the vast majority of American leaders ever since—to use a convenient as well as causative event—Frederick Jackson Turner formulated the frontier thesis in 1893.

Beginning with the proposition that "a prosperous business community is the measure of our performance," Kennedy moved directly to support such overseas economic expansion. "I therefore favor expansion of our foreign trade and private investments abroad." "Our exports," he warned, "have not been large enough." He did enter one reservation to the general axiom about expansion, but it did *not* concern the unfavorable effects of such expansion on America's relations with the rest of the world. It involved only the problem of expanding in such a way as to "avoid serious adverse effects on domestic industry that can arise from foreign competition."

Like his predecessors, Kennedy projected this economic expansionism into the political, strategic, and ideological spheres. "Now in 1960, American frontiers are on the Rhine and the Mekong and Tigris and the Euphrates and the Amazon. There is no place in the world that is not of concern to all of us. . . . We are responsible for the maintenance of freedom all around the world." "The cause of all mankind," he cried, "is the cause of America." This approach defined power and the future in terms of a struggle with the evil of the Soviet Union and other Communist societies. "Now the question is whether the world will exist half free and half slave, and if it does not, which way it will go." "My campaign for the Presidency, therefore, is an effort to mobilize the great strength . . . for the great struggle."

Policy toward Cuba became one of the main examples of the way that Kennedy integrated these personal, economic, and ideological themes. The issue also revealed that Kennedy was aware that there were problems of morality and legality as well as of power and expansion and righteousness. One of the most suggestive indicators of Kennedy's entire outlook was provided by a story concerning Cuba that he told time and again throughout the campaign. Little comment is needed. The way Kennedy changed the story by dropping all reservations about whether it was right for America to control so much of Cuban life indicates Kennedy's underlying approach to resolving the tension between power and morality.

August 24: "Three years ago I went to Havana. I was told that the American Ambassador was the second most powerful man in Cuba. Probably he should not be, but he is not today."

September 2: "I visited Havana 3 years ago and I was informed that the American Ambassador was the second most influential man in Cuba. He is not today. . . . This is the problem that we face in 1960."

September 5: "Three years ago I went to Havana, Cuba, and I was told that the American Ambassador was the second most powerful man in Cuba. I am not saying he should have been, but he was."

September 15: "I was in Havana 3 years ago. The American Ambassador informed me on that occasion that he was the second most powerful and influential man in Cuba. Today the American Ambassador is not."

September 20: "Three years ago when I was in Cuba, the American Ambassador was the second most influential man in Cuba. Today the Soviet Ambassador is."

Kennedy's first major speech on Cuba, by which he injected the subject into the forefront of the campaign, was delivered on October 6, 1960. It contained all the basic elements of his analysis and policy recommendations. But he had termed Cuba "a fundamental question in foreign policy" as early as September 6, and the following reconstruction of his views includes quotations from all relevant speeches.

It is noteworthy, first of all, that Kennedy's sense of historical development was limited to the six years prior to the fall of Batista. That was the period during which what he termed the "most serious errors"—or "the basic errors"—were made. He did mention, once, in this connection, the failure "to help Cuba meet its desperate need for economic development." But even then he limited the reference to the same brief period. He was more concerned with the failure to use American power to force Batista to step down in order to block Castro; and his argument suggests—but does not prove—that he was aware of Pawley's plan of December, 1958, to employ that technique. Kennedy's only reference to an earlier phase of American-Cuban relations involved a highly inaccurate and romanticized version of Roosevelt's policy during the 1930's.

The situation in 1960, according to Kennedy, was "critical"—"a disaster." Cuba was "so dangerous" because it represented "the first time in the history of the United States" that "an enemy stands poised at the throat of the United States." Even by the most generous of judgments, this was a gross historical boner. Napoleon stood there in the early years of the 19th century, and Castro is not yet to be compared to Napoleon. Kennedy's argument, of course, was that Cuba was "a new satellite" of the Soviet Union. But he was again gravely inaccurate in describing the island as "a Communist base of operations a few minutes from our coast—by jet plane, missile or submarine." The only foreign base in Cuba was—and remains —the American naval base.

Kennedy's extreme attack prompted the Eisenhower Administration, probably at the insistence of Nixon, to institute export controls over American trade with Cuba. Kennedy dismissed the action as "too little and too late." His program was to plan "more stringent economic sanctions," to assure the Cubans through a massive propaganda campaign that they would again be free, and to give encouragement and aid to those "who are leading the resistance to Castro"—to those "who offer eventual hope of overthrowing Castro." After all, Kennedy argued, "if you can't stand up to Castro, how can you be expected to stand up to Khrushchev?"

All of this was to be done, however, without breaking American laws or Inter-American treaties. "I have never advocated and I do not now advocate," he asserted unequivocally on October 23, "intervention in Cuba in violation of our treaty obligations." But as so subtly yet convincingly indicated in his telling of the story about the American Ambassador being once but no longer the second most powerful man in Cuba, Kennedy violated his pledge of morality in order to honor his concern for power, his externalization of evil, and his urge to control the future while still in the present.

When Kennedy authorized the invasion, he knowingly violated his avowed morality. In perhaps the single most perceptive and courageous action of his distinguished career, Senator Fulbright bluntly told the President that he was mistaken on moral and pragmatic grounds. He did this not once, but twice. Fulbright's performance was a magnificent display of statesmanship—both absolutely and by comparison with the performance of such liberals as presidential assistant Arthur M. Schlesinger, Jr. As with others, Schlesinger in the crisis valued his future influence more than his present morality. Schlesinger's failure is particularly striking because he has so diligently and haughtily criticized the Communists for just that scale of values—and also because he has stressed the moral issue of slavery in explaining the coming of the American Civil War.

The failure of American leadership was dramatized even

more terribly by the failure of Adlai Stevenson to resign his post as Ambassador to the United Nations. Stevenson is a bigger man by far than Schlesinger, Jr. He also stressed morality and responsibility in both his presidential campaigns. Stevenson wept after discovering that he had been lied to so that he would lie to the world. And he apparently gave President Kennedy a verbal thrashing that left the younger man temporarily chastened. But Stevenson went back to his office. Unlike Jefferson, a man he was fond of quoting, Stevenson could not bring himself to resign even with a view to future leadership.

The most perceptive and sobering comment on the American-instigated invasion of Cuba, and upon the conduct of the overwhelming majority of American leaders, was written many years ago by a superb novelist and a profound commentator on human affairs named Joseph Conrad.

"Most of us," Conrad wrote, "if you will pardon me for betraying the universal secret, have, at some time or other, discovered in ourselves a readiness to stray far, ever so far, on the wrong road."

Perhaps it is expecting too much for Americans to thank Castro for offering them an opportunity to learn that lesson. But they should seize the day and do so. They must do so if they are not to stray even further on the wrong road.

12

The Lessons Waiting to Be Learned

Almost three-quarters of a century has now elapsed since the United States began seriously and continually to intervene to set limits upon, and to control, Cuban development. The most appropriate commentary on that performance, at least for Americans who still honor the ideas and ideals of the Declaration of Independence, was made by Robert Burns in his poem *To The Reverend John M'Math*.

God knows, I'm no the thing I should
   be,
Nor am I even the thing I could be.

Even President Kennedy once remarked that there is a lesson in this for all of us. The trouble with such learning by doing, however, is that the experience may be so painful and embarrassing that it aborts the learning process itself. There is considerable evidence that this has happened to a good many Americans in the Cuban situation. Evasions, distortions, rationalizations, and outright falsehoods have played, and continue to play, a very large and influential role in the analysis and discussion of the subject. And as far as policy is concerned, we are still waiting for Castro "to go through the wringer." We still insist, moreover, and in spite of all our noble talk about morality, that the Cuban people accompany him on that painful journey.

The principal lesson of the Cuban course in adult education is the one that Thomas Henry Huxley described so well in 1877. "Perhaps the most valuable result of all education is the ability to make yourself do the thing you have to do, when it ought to be done, whether you like it or not; it is the first lesson that ought to be learned; and however early a man's training begins, it is probably the last lesson that he learns thoroughly."

What we have to do, if we are to avoid similar disasters in the future (and perhaps the very near future), is to face up to five specific lessons to be learned from our dealings with Cuba since 1895. This ought to be done now, however much we may prefer to avoid the unpleasantness involved, because we need to do so and because the time is short.

First. The lesson of United States responsibility.

This responsibility takes several forms of a general and specific nature. The United States instigated and fought to a successful conclusion the first modern revolution for independence from a colonial empire. We are, at least in this sense, the exemplar of the anti-colonial and anti-imperialist movement. We have pitted and tarnished that reputation by our actions throughout the world since at least as early as 1895, and by our conduct toward Cuba in particular, but the United States is still a model and an image of that kind of revolution. We have a clear moral obligation to support and assist such revolutions— even when they are staged against our power and influence. Indeed, particularly when they are waged against us.

This broad kind of responsibility also exists in connection with the United States as an industrial nation of enormous power and wealth. We have consistently and insistently presented ourselves as *the* wonder of the modern world, whose goals and methods should be followed by all other societies. For that matter, we have often asserted that they must follow our example if they are to avoid the most terrible consequences. Considered in terms of either imperative thus offered the poor and developing countries—the moral or the logical—the United States has created for itself an obligation to facilitate the efforts of countries that manifest a desire to emulate its achievement.

These considerations are particularly relevant to the case of Cuba. The United States first took the island and controlled it as a colony, then placed it in a semi-colonial condition, and finally created an economic relationship that accomplished the essential political and social as well as economic purposes of colonialism without the embarrassments and troublesome administrative problems connected with the traditional pattern. As an integral part of that relationship, moreover, the United States encouraged Cuba to think of its own future in terms of the American standard of living. The United States was not only responsible for the conditions that produced Castro, but for the broad objectives of the Revolution itself.

Finally, and in the narrower and more explicit sense, the United States bears the responsibility for two kinds of intervention against Castro's Revolution. It first chose not to help Castro except on its own, unilaterally determined, conditions. It refused to supply such assistance with a clear—even brilliant —understanding of the consequences that its decision would produce. Then the United States planned, financed, and directed a military action designed to destroy the Castro government and replace it with one extensively dependent upon American favor. In both cases, furthermore, the United States knew and accepted the fact that its action would bring additional death, pain, and suffering to the Cuban people. This grave responsibility cannot be mitigated by saying that no American combat units fired upon Cubans. That claim may actually be false. But even if it is valid, it remains true that American policy has caused—and continues to cause—death, pain, and suffering to the population of Cuba.

Second. The lesson that revolutions are dynamic, not static.

This seems in some respects to be the truth that most Americans have the greatest difficulty in grasping. One is constantly and ever more strongly impressed, in reading the newspaper and magazine accounts (and in reviewing oral commentary) on the Cuban Revolution, with the extent to which Americans assumed that the Revolution should—as well as would—end with the defeat of Batista. While it is too much

157

to say that Americans were truly surprised by the idea of a revolution that aimed to change the old order, it is not too much to say that they were rapidly and increasingly perplexed and annoyed that the Cuban revolutionaries meant to make fundamental changes, and intended to go ahead with their program in the face of opposition and criticism.

One suspects, in the end, that this is one of the unfavorable results—one of the costs—of being first. It has been so long since we had a revolution that we are very much out of touch with that rudimentary feature of political and social reality. This is true even if one views the Civil War, at least in some respects, as a revolution. One hundred years—let alone two centuries—is a long time between revolutions. No other major country in the world has been tucked away in a cocoon for anything approaching that length of time. (England is *not* an exception because the British Empire has experienced many colonial uprisings which involved not only the politics—but also the people—of the British Isles.)

We seem to have forgotten, furthermore, some mundane but nevertheless essential features of our own revolutions. They lasted a long time (1774-1789, and 1860-1876); they were violent and bloody, and those who opposed them suffered great losses up to and including their lives; they were affected by the attitudes and policies of foreign countries; and some of the avowed objectives of the revolutions—such as the emancipation of the Negro—have still not been achieved. All of these considerations are directly relevant to our attitudes and behavior toward the Cuban Revolution. One has the distinct impression, for example, that most Americans considered it something of a personal affront as well as a general insult that the Cubans had the gall to take their politics so seriously. And we have judged and condemned the Revolution long before it is even completed—let alone before its fruits have blossomed and matured. It is like judging a child for life at the end of a particularly bad week during adolescence, and proceeding ever afterward to act upon that judgment.

Each of these features of a revolution could be examined in considerable detail. Perhaps it is time, for that matter, for some talented historian or social critic to reacquaint the American people with the facts of life about revolutions per se. To provide, as it were, a poverty-guns-and-ideas version of the birds-and-the-bees story. A simple, blunt book on that subject might have vastly more positive consequences for American foreign policy than all the explanations and analyses of Communism and foreign aid that have been written since 1945.

Such an undertaking is clearly beyond the scope of this essay, but it is necessary to discuss two characteristics of revolutions that have a particularly direct connection with American thought and action concerning Cuba and Castro. It is essential to understand, and to think and act in terms of, the truth that a revolution is not a struggle for desirable but deferrable fringe benefits. A revolution is a battle over and about and for the fundamental structure, substance, direction, and tone of the society itself. Revolutions are made by men who care deeply about basic issues and who are driven into action by their commitment.

Hence it is largely irrelevant to belabor them for caring so much that they refuse to give up the revolution either because we want them to in order to make our life less difficult, or because some of their actions contradict ideas or ideals they proclaim as part of the revolution. In the first place, most revolutionaries—and most certainly Castro among them—are intensely aware of this problem. Indeed, much of their wild rhetoric is produced by the tension that results from their awareness. An intense consciousness of the odds on failure is the very texture of their existence.

In the second place, it is childish—if not simply dishonest—to pretend for the purposes of making severe judgments as though fundamental changes can be brought about without painful costs. If one began, for example, with the year 1876 and added up all the deaths and other harsh and desperate human costs that it took to win—finally—the routine, functioning acceptance of unions, and the installation of safety devices, in either mining or railroading, one would discover that even non-revolutionary changes come at an extremely high price. Yet we in America have judged Castro as though the United States moved from the conditions of 1776 to those of 1962 through a process of joyful goodwill and immaculate rationality. The point of this lesson about revolutions is that the truly moral and intelligent objectives for outsiders involve help to reduce those costs to the lowest possible level—not demands that the revolution be abandoned, or sermons about evil men who refuse to give up their mistaken goals.

Another central feature of social revolutions is that they are made by coalitions. This means that conflict is built into the revolutionary government that takes power on the morrow of victory. Just such a coalition started and fought the American Revolution, and governed the new nation during the period from 1783 to 1786. By 1785, however, that coalition was dividing into rival blocs over the questions of policy toward the West and the need and desirability of a stronger central government. Violent personal antagonisms developed, extremist and abusive language became the vernacular of political debate, secession was seriously considered both in the North and the South, and at one point (in the 1790's) civil war seemed to many men a distinct probability.

A similar, and far more violent and embittered, conflict took place inside the Bolshevik Revolution. To think of Soviet politics as being monolithic is like thinking of the atom as being a teeny-weeny marble. The fight between Stalin and Trotsky was merely the most famous of such battles within Russia. In the middle 1920's, for example, a serious and extremely significant debate over the means and tempo of industrialization, and the way to handle the agricultural problem, engaged all elements of the Communist Party and set the pattern of Soviet development for two decades.

As these two disparate examples indicate, it is very misleading in two crucial respects to think about revolutions as being either wholly democratic or wholly non-democratic. Such a difference exists in theory, and it is approached in practice. But that either-or approach distorts reality by substituting a choice between abstract and polarized opposites for what is actually the problem of estimating the degree of representative government, and of evaluating the direction and momentum toward or away from that objective. This judgment has to be made, furthermore, in terms of a revolution—not in terms of evolutionary changes occurring within a fundamentally stable framework.

Professor Frank Tannenbaum of Columbia University, certainly one of the world's most perceptive students of Latin America, has made this point in such a striking way that it deserves verbatim repetition:

"The distance that separates the poor or the peasant on the plantation and the rancho from the cultured and wealthy that govern the country is so wide that it is difficult to think of how it can be bridged or, even narrowed. For unless the favored of fortune and the poor, who in most countries are very poor, achieve some broader basis of identity, democratic government must remain an aspiration or an illusion. . . .

"There is no easy path to the encouragement of democratic government or to its certain emergence. . . .

"In Latin America I am certain that social reform must precede the effort to develop democratic ways. . . .

"If the proposal to support democratic growth in Latin America is taken seriously, then we would have to support an agrarian program."

These remarks have a direct bearing on the entire question of revolutionary coalitions in general, and on the one in Cuba in particular. A coalition that develops to overthrow an existing

161

Latin American government falls into one of two broad categories. It can be, and often has been, a coalition dominated and controlled by men (and elements) which desire to clean up or reform a system that is being warped or abused by a dictator or a small elite. Such a revolutionary coalition is fundamentally upper-class in composition and outlook. Moderate and radical elements may join it, and even exert some sporadic influence on its policies, but they never control it.[1] What there is of a middle class—and American commentators manifest a great propensity to exaggerate its size as well as its power—is accepted into such a coalition with fewer reservations, and it may even be given certain rewards, but it is not allowed to control either the coalition or the revolution. Its gains are incidental, and as yet have never been significant enough to enable it to initiate, control, and win the next revolution.

There have been other examples, but certainly Castro's Revolution is the prime illustration of a revolutionary coalition led and dominated by men who define the revolution in terms of, and seek support from, "the poor or the peasant on the plantation and the rancho." The nature of this kind of coalition is quite different. Here the upper-class members are tolerated as long as they support the revolution, but even under those conditions they are not offered rewards *as members of the upper class*. They do benefit from the revolution to the extent that they identify with the aspirations of the general population of the society, and may in fact gain certain guaranteed social services. Actually, it is possible for such upper-class citizens to benefit more in psychic terms from a lower-class revolution than the lower class can gain in psychic *or* real terms from an upper-class revolution.

Middle-class members of a revolutionary coalition con-

---

1. If this seems strange or contradictory, one has only to think of the men who made the American Revolution. Most of them were class conscious aristocrats: Washington, Mason, Adams, and Jay are enough names to make the point.

trolled by men intent upon a radical reconstruction of society are again given secondary consideration. They win less from such a revolution than from the kind led and controlled by the upper class. The reason for this is that a radical revolution views the middle class from below, and therefore sees it as a tacit or overt ally of the upper class. And it often is.

Third. The lesson that we live in a volatile world in which most of the revolutions are occurring in societies which lack a powerful middle class.

This means, in the first place, that any effort to encourage and support middle-class revolutions amounts to an artificial forcing of history. That can be done—if at all—only through the direct and sustained use of force. To put it bluntly, such middle-class revolutions are minority revolutions which have no general basis of power in the poor society itself, and hence have to be assisted and supported by American power.

It also means, and this is often overlooked, that the forcing of such middle-class revolutions upon a society not ready for them tends to increase the probability, and to accelerate the time table, of a lower-class revolution which will be even more radical and more violent than if it came to power at the present time. It is this consideration which gives meaning to the paradoxical remark, put most neatly by Herbert L. Matthews of the *New York Times,* that the most fortunate thing about the American invasion of Cuba was that it failed. Had it succeeded in establishing a middle-class group in power, the result would have been either a prolonged period of American armed intervention or a truly orgiastic upheaval against the American-installed government.

Finally, the propensity to think and act in terms of middle-class revolutions is very apt to produce extremely frustrating results. The assumption is, of course, that such revolutions will usher in a period of stability, of law and order, and of pro-Americanism. But premature middle-class revolutions are inherently unstable. For one thing, control of the government becomes the object of a contest between the elites in command of the various functional segments of the middle class. And the small operational base of the middle class invites upper-class coups and lower-class rebellions. Either of these developments may occur, as they are presently doing in Argentina, Brazil, and Venezuela. But, even if they do not (or if they are repressed), the middle class has to bid for support from its rivals. In any case, American expectations are seldom fulfilled.

All these considerations combine to suggest that the American choice lies between three alternatives: the United States can support upper-class, conservative revolutions, it can support and assist lower-class revolutions, or it can stay out of the situation and permit the various elements within the societies in question to proceed with their own struggles and revolutions in their own way. Whatever the decision on that matter, it cannot be made intelligently save in the context of the next lesson of the Cuban experience.

Fourth. The lesson that we cannot think intelligently or effectively about the present so long as we do so in terms of the past. One of the crucial values of studying history is that it helps us learn what to forget because it is irrelevant or misleading. Such things are of course part of history, and cannot be erased, but they do not provide significant insights into either the past or the present.

We cannot, that is to say, consider the option of supporting upper-class revolutions on the assumption that the upper class in poor and developing societies is comparable either with our own upper-class Founding Fathers, or with the best and most socially conscious and responsible of our existing leaders. The reason for this is simple: they are generally not comparable. This is not meant as a personal slur on any individuals. It is meant as a historical and sociological judgment. There are exceptions, but the basic proposition remains valid.

America's Founding Fathers were the product of two centuries of development involving a tradition of upper-class responsibility and training, and of an unparalleled opportunity to exploit the economic and political advantages of a fabulously wealthy continent separated from the seat of empire by 3,000 miles in an age of sailing vessels.

Upper-class leaders in Latin America, and in most other poor areas, have simply not enjoyed those remarkably favorable circumstances. Their original traditions of *noblesse oblige* have atrophied, and they have been watched over and controlled with all the efficiency of a world intimately bound together by instantaneous communications and highly mobile striking forces with great fire power. To support this group means to continue such controls while educating its members to modern standards of a socially conscious upper class. It would involve turning the government itself into a trade school modeled on Harvard, Annapolis, and the Chicago (or Wharton) School of Business. And that is a project to think about very carefully and soberly before undertaking it.

Neither can the United States consider the alternative of supporting radical, lower-class revolutions as though it were a problem of repeating the New Deal in foreign lands while avoiding the participation of Communists. *We are simply not living in the 1930's any longer.*

To begin with, the New Deal did not solve any structural problems in the United States, and it is basically irrelevant to the conditions, circumstances, and aspirations of the poor countries at the present time. Those societies are struggling to throw off the vestiges of feudalism and colonialism, and to build the foundations and framework of an independent country with a balanced, dynamic political economy. The New Deal was an approach to saving and reforming a mature industrial capitalism. And it did not succeed by its own fundamental criteria of generating prosperity and social equity under conditions of peace. One would be far better off, at least in this rudimentary respect of finding an earlier model for the poor countries to emulate, to go back to the British mercantilists of the 17th and 18th centuries. Or to Americans of the period between 1785 and 1828. After all, Albert Gallatin and John Quincy Adams had Five Year Plans long before the Russians even had any Bolsheviks.

This might even be helpful in connection with the problem of evolving a mature attitude toward radical dissenters. The Puritans, who were in the beginning as doctrinaire, bigoted, and ruthless as the Communists of a later period, turned out to be extremely valuable mercantilists and state builders once they were accepted as members of the community. There is nothing quite as effective as exclusion to create and nourish extremism.

It is simply not true to say, as Draper and others do, that Communism and Communists do not change. They are changing all the time. If one really holds the view that Communists cannot and do not modify their thinking and change their programs, then there is really nothing to do but bury down in a shelter-centered garrison state and get it over with.

Nor will it do to call people "new" Communists, as Draper does, even though they are not actually Communists but only radicals collaborating with Communists inside a coalition. Or to refuse to draw a clear line between men who are inspired and guided by Marx but who are not Communists in terms of Stalin's Russia or Mao's China. This is to destroy even the *possibility* of supporting lower-class revolutions. And to destroy alternatives on false grounds is the height of anti-intellectualism. It is also to block off as being evil a policy that could very well open up an era of vast and exciting development within such poor and backward societies—and of much better relations with them. Yet that is precisely the result of thinking about radical lower-class revolutions in terms of the 1930's and the Soviet Union. It is a highly dangerous fixation shared by conservatives and liberals as well as ex-radicals.

Finally, it is very misleading to think about keeping our hands off the revolutions in the poorer countries as though that course involved a return to what is called isolationism. Since the United States has been actively involved in world affairs— has been a world power—ever since it broke away from the British Empire, it is very questionable whether the term isolationism has any usefulness whatsoever. If it has any meaning, however, it is in connection with the refusal of the United States to join the League of Nations in 1919, and with the reluctance of the nation to take strong action leading to war against the Axis Powers in the middle and later 1930's. Yet throughout that period from 1919 to 1941 the United States carried on a very active diplomacy in all parts of the world.

But even if we admit that such a specific and restricted definition of isolationism has some validity, it still has no relevance in connection with a discussion of the proper policy toward revolutions in underdeveloped countries in the second half of the century. The idea behind restraining oneself toward such revolutions does not even imply breaking off diplomatic relations, let alone ignoring the nation in question. It simply means allowing the society to have its revolution and then working out an appropriate relationship with the new society and its government. As far as the problem of the nationalization of American property is concerned, the American taxpayer is already paying for insurance to cover such crises.

This policy of restraint is the most demanding of all the possible approaches toward revolutions. This is true even in cases where the revolutions do not impinge upon the vital national interests of the United States. We are caught up in a pattern of thinking which externalizes good as well as evil. Hence we assume we have to control everything—events that do not threaten our welfare and safety just as well as those that do have a negative impact on our national interests.

The result is an inability to leave anything alone anywhere in the world. Internationalism has become intermeddling. We have defined our business as coterminous with every crossroad in the world. By that definition, minding one's own business becomes a process of minding the world. We are more than a little bit like the parent who cannot let go of the child as it approaches and crosses the threshold into adulthood. Such parents have lived vicariously through their children to the extent that letting the child go means giving up a major part of the meaning of their own adult life. We have defined so much of America in terms of the world that we are afraid to allow the world to develop in a pluralistic manner. Yet this is precisely what we must do if we are to retain any of our self-respect, and even any of our opportunity to build the kind of an America that we are capable of creating.

Indeed, we have been so busy thinking about the world that we have done very little thinking about the United States. And it shows in the state of the nation—and the society.

Fifth. The lesson that the place to begin is by changing our present policy toward Cuba. In a sense, of course, the act of changing policy is not a beginning but a culmination; it represents a learning of the other, less explicit and visible, lessons that the history of American-Cuban relations offers for our consideration. History itself does not teach anything. History merely offers a way for people to learn by reflecting upon the record and the inter-relationships of what they have done. And learning of that kind is notably difficult because it involves both the admission that we have not always been intelligent or moral, and the will to adjust our behavior accordingly.

This lesson involving a change of policy is made still more demanding by the continuing changes in Cuba itself, and in the relationship between Cuba, the United States, and the Soviet Union. But neither American policy-makers nor the public at large can expect reality to stand still while they pull even with it at their leisure—or assume that one or two acts will stabilize or tranquilize the situation. Any significant change of policy involves a period of time during which the new approach seems to produce little or no improvement. The disappointments and frustrations of that period have to be understood and endured with patience and understanding; otherwise the reaction back toward a harsher version of the old policy will produce even more serious trouble.

The events of the spring and summer of 1962 serve to illustrate these difficulties. Castro's persistent efforts to strengthen the position of the 26th July Movement within its coalition with the Cuban Communists were dramatized early in the year by his effective attack on the Communist leader Anibal Escalante. Escalante left the country, and others who had sympathized with or supported him also lost their positions. These developments coincided with a reassessment of the campaign to move Cubans into agricultural cooperatives and a decision to return some land to individual ownership and cultivation, and with renewed overtures by Castro for a rapprochement with the United States. His basic proposal, to negotiate compensation for American property that had been nationalized in return for renewed American sugar purchases, seems in fact to have been in the process of being considered by the State Department in June. But American policy-makers were not ready to act. Had they been, it seems possible that the opening might have led to a decrease in tension and a slow improvement of relations.

Such a rapprochement might have proceeded rapidly enough, if the United States had been prepared to move promptly, to have provided Castro and the Revolution with an alternate way of coping with their difficulties. These troubles were partly inherent in the development of the Revolution, partly the consequence of past and existing American policy, and partly the result of what many informed observers have called the worst drought in at least 40 years. Castro needed general and continuing economic assistance in reorganizing the Cuban economy and short-run aid to meet the immediate crisis. And, *so long as the United States did not give any firm indication that it was going to modify or change its policy,* Castro had to act on the assumption that he required more military support.

Given the failure of the United States to move quickly to meet his overtures, Castro turned again to the Soviet Union. The Russians began to pour in the help that he requested. In the short run, that only increased the tension. This took two forms. First, it made it increasingly difficult for Castro and other non-Communist Cuban radicals to maintain, let alone improve, their position vis-à-vis the Cuban Communists inside the government. American policy thus had the practical effect of subverting its own avowed objectives; or, at any rate, of making it ever more difficult to achieve those objectives short of a recourse to general violence. Secondly, the extremely militant reaction in the United States during September, 1962, recalled the similar outbursts of invasion talk during the fall of 1897 and the spring of 1898. Much of the rhetoric even sounded as though it had been lifted from the newspapers and the *Congressional Record* of that earlier period and reused after merely substituting Russia for Spain.

And it might be that the result, at least in some respects, would turn out to be similar. The United States might indeed invade Cuba in order to be done with Castro and the Revolution. It is misleading, however, to think solely in terms of such direct military intervention by American forces. The non-military pressure exerted by the United States on Castro and Cuban society has been and is enormous. It is wholly possible, for example, for the direct and indirect encouragement and assistance given Castro's opponents to create a grave crisis. The murder of Castro, to consider but one possibility, would very probably lead to a period of horrible violence and destruction. Whether the Cuban Communists won out, or whether some anti-Castro coalition emerged victorious, the cost paid by Cuban society would be immense. Even the latter result, while superficially a triumph for American policy, would of necessity involve the United States in prolonged intervention to re-establish and maintain order, and to restore the economy. (The money spent on an operation of that kind would very probably have been

170

more than enough to tide Castro and the Revolution over the crisis of 1959.) This possibility, and all the other variations imaginable, have to be considered as direct consequences of the American decision in 1959 to "let Castro go through the wringer."

The Soviets had certainly anticipated a strong negative reaction when they decided to aid Castro in an extensive way, but it might be that they had underestimated both its vigor and its duration. In that case, an American operation against Castro —direct or indirect—would very probably touch off Communist action in the Middle East, in Asia, and perhaps even in Europe. A general nuclear war could be the final result.

Hence the problem remains the same as it was before the events of 1962. The circumstances have become increasingly difficult, delicate, and dangerous, but the need is still to change American policy. Action could proceed along three lines. First, the United States could begin, on its own, to re-establish direct communication with Castro and to open discussions pointing toward an agreement on sugar and compensation for American property owners, and toward formal recognition.

Second, America and Russia could initiate talks with the idea of using Cuba to effect a general breakthrough on controlled and inspected disarmament. The Russian position in Cuba, for example, and the American position in Turkey, could be phased-out in parallel operations. The opportunity to use third countries to begin continuously controlled and inspected disarmament offers an almost unique opportunity to defuse the Cold War. For, up to September 1962, the United States enjoyed a wholly unmatched position of strength around the borders of the Soviet Union. The Soviet Union had nothing to compare with the system of American military bases around the perimeter of Russia.

It is quite true, of course, that aid to Cuba did not create such a system for Russia. To be fully comparable with the American position in Turkey, the Soviets would have to move

Cuba northward some 125 miles and fit it in along the Florida coast, build bomber and missile bases manned and controlled by Red Army and Air Force personnel, undertake routine reconnaissance operations involving radio, radar, and aircraft (U-2 flights along the border from Miami to San Diego), and supply still more technicians. But the opportunity to *prevent* such literal parity between Turkey and Cuba would seem to be even more attractive than an opening to negotiate the withdrawal of such equal Soviet power after it existed.

Third, and dependent to some degree upon the evolution of the kind of negotiations suggested, the United States and Russia could work out an agreement to define Cuba in terms of Finland. Both superpowers would accept limits on their action in Cuba, and both would supply economic assistance. It is conceivable, in this respect, that Cuba could become the showplace of coexistence. It has the resources, and such an agreement would make it possible to develop them peacefully.

These suggestions are meant to emphasize the point that there are non-violent approaches to the Cuban situation which do not involve any danger to the national security of the United States. They by no means exhaust the possibilities for such positive action. But whatever form the approach might take, the broad significance of the crisis that developed in the fall of 1962 would seem to be apparent. It is time for us Americans to stop living in the past and to find out whether we are up to coping with the present in a peaceful, creative manner.

Postscript

The events which occurred after the completion of this manuscript in September, 1962, and particularly those beginning with President Kennedy's speech of October 22nd announcing a blockade of shipping to Cuba, serve only to emphasize and dramatize the central line of argument advanced in the body of this essay.

There would be no missiles of any description or range in Cuba if the actions of the United States toward Cuba since 1898 had followed and honored its professions and promises.

As was pointed out in the closing passages of the essay as completed in September, the United States faced at that time a fateful choice. It could change its policy or risk being confronted in Cuba with a situation comparable with the one posed for the Soviet Union by American power in such countries as Turkey, Formosa, and Okinawa.

The Kennedy administration did not change its policy. It did *not* respond to Cuban overtures for negotiation. It did *not* relax its economic, political, and military pressure on Cuba. It did *not* stop the provocative and harrassing actions of anti-Castro exiles in the United States. It did *not,* in short, honor either its own neutrality laws or its obligations under international treaties.

Furthermore, the Kennedy administration did *not* initiate quiet, serious discussions with the Soviet Union designed to reach an accomodation whereby an American agreement to tolerate the Cuban Revolution would be matched by a Russian commitment to halt its military aid to the Castro Government. And, in what was perhaps the act that revealed most about its own character, the Kennedy administration did *not* go to the American public with a candid review of American responsibility for the situation in Cuba, and of the resulting crisis vis-à-vis the Soviet Union, and with a statement of quiet confidence in the ability of the people of the United States to match the restraint and maturity of Soviet citizens during the years they have been confronted with American bombers and missiles but a few minutes flight-time across Russian borders.

Instead, the Kennedy administration acted unilaterally, and in a manner calculated to dramatize the situation, to establish itself as the sole and arbitrary gate-keeper of all international shipping bound for Cuba. This was by all codes and interpretations of international law an act of war.

The resulting crisis could produce any, or a combination, of several consequences: a nuclear holocaust, a series of American air strikes against targets in Cuba, an all-out American invasion of Cuba, conventional warfare in other areas of the world, or an informal or formal settlement of the Cuban crisis through negotiation. Any effort as of October 24 to predict the specific outcome would be as irrelevant to the purpose of this essay as it would be to the policy decisions being taken by the governments involved in the crisis.

There are three kinds of issues, however, that can be raised by an author whose book will be published approximately six weeks after he scribbles his last word. The first is to point out that American actions of the kind taken by Kennedy toward Cuba have repeatedly offered the Soviet Union an opportunity to finesse the situation against the United States. The usual argument for confronting the Russians with an ultimatum of the kind exemplified by the embargo of October 23-24, 1962, is that it forces them to back down and thereby saves the peace and prevents future crises. But this logic overlooks the truth that the Soviet Union, by reacting with overtures for negotiation and accomodation, immediately preempts the role of the peacemaker. This in turn undercuts the American argument that the Soviet Union is responsible for all the trouble and tension in the world, places the United States on the defensive by having to respond to peaceful alternatives framed by Russia, and ultimately weakens the initial support given America by other countries. The recourse to unilateral, extreme, and bellicose measures offers evidence only about the leaders who employ them, and raises basic questions about the character of that leadership.

If the crisis engendered by such actions does lead to war, then the responsibility is by no means so clearly fixed upon the Russians as the advocates of such a policy maintain. The reason for this involves the second main point that can be made, regardless of the outcome of the crisis. Despite the rhetoric of the Kennedy administration, missiles are by definition neither offensive nor defensive. A military missile is a high velocity vehicle designed to deliver a warhead on a target. It is offensive if it is used to initiate an attack. It is defensive if it is fired in response to an assault. Missiles are disturbing, it is true, but the feeling induced by their presence exists independently of when they are fired, for the simple reason that they cause the death and the damage in any event.

But the act of defining a missile as offensive before it is used to initiate an attack is a wholly arbitrary and unilateral action. By taking this step, the Kennedy administration has in effect retaliated before any blow has been struck. This standard justifies Soviet action of a similar kind. The point is important not because it will save any lives if war results, but because it is vital to understand the logic of American policy. From being almost obsessed with fear of another Pearl Harbor, the United States under the Kennedy Administration has moved perilously close to adopting the psychology that produced that attack.

Finally, an author, confronted with a book going to press in the midst of such a crisis, can attempt to define and clarify the crucial factors upon which any analysis and judgment of the issue must depend. These would seem to be the following:

First. The United States enjoyed and exercised, directly and indirectly, preponderant power in Cuba from 1898 until the summer of 1962. The Soviet Union neither caused nor assisted

Castro's Revolution of 1958-1959. The rise of Russian influence in Cuba has been the result of the failure of American policy.

Second. American reaction to increased Russian influence in Cuba has been wholly consistent with the double standard of diplomacy first enunciated in the Monroe Doctrine in 1823. This point should not be confused with the question of whether or not the Monroe Doctrine is still relevant in an age of ICBM's. That is a pseudo-issue which has the effect of obscuring the heart of the matter. The real point about the Monroe Doctrine is that its double standard of judgment has never provided—and does not now provide—a valid moral or pragmatic foundation for a foreign policy.

In the same speech in which he declared the Western Hemisphere off-limits to European powers, President James Monroe openly and officially threw the weight and influence of the United States government on the side of European revolutions against the status quo.[1]

This double standard has been followed by almost every administration since the time of Monroe. And until now, at any rate, it has been the basis of the policy of the Kennedy administration toward Cuba. But tradition does not make morality. It only makes custom. American policy as exemplified in the Monroe Doctrine is based on a double standard dependent solely upon force for any recognition it may obtain.

Third. President Kennedy's assertion on October 22, 1962, that Russian military aid to Cuba upset the precarious balance of power between the United States and the Soviet Union is false. The charge will not stand up under the weight of facts that have been known publicly for at least a year prior to Kennedy's speech.

There did exist, during the late 1950's, a kind of balance of strength between the United States and the Soviet Union. The

---

1. The documentary evidence for this is in my volume, *The Shaping of American Diplomacy* (Chicago, Rand McNally Co., 1956; paperback edition 1962), pp. 160-161.

United States then enjoyed, as it had since the end of World War II (and as it still does), a vast superiority in nuclear power and in the capacity to deliver that power on target in Russia. The Soviet Union, on the other hand, had managed to conceal the main elements of its nuclear capacity, which in quantitative terms was far inferior. This secrecy, a classic weapon in military strategy, gave the Soviets the potential ability to strike back against the far greater nuclear strength of the United States.

Unilateral American action destroyed this balance. The U-2 flights provided American officials with extensive and reliable information on Soviet nuclear bases. This meant that the United States had the potential to destroy—with the first American attack—the Russian ability to retaliate. Having lost their strategic secrecy, the Russians had only a far weaker nuclear arsenal, and delivery system, with which to confront the awesome power of the United States.

The Russians responded by undertaking nuclear tests to prove-out weapons—such as the 50 megaton bomb, and other warheads that could be launched by smaller, more mobile missiles—that would restore some measure of balance with the United States. Russian military aid to Cuba was another part of the effort undertaken in response to the U-2 flights, and to the American decision to base its nuclear strategy on the ability to destroy Russian missile emplacements in a first attack. By seeking to attain the illusory goal of perfect security, the United States had only moved closer to war.

Fourth. American responsibility for the very great economic and political pressure on the Cuban people, including official encouragement of anti-Castro action, antedates any Soviet influence on the Cuban Revolution. The decision to put Castro "through the wringer" was made in Washington between March and June, 1959. It was made without any reference to Soviet influence in Cuba. *For that matter, it was made with the clear realization that it might increase Communist influence.* The moral responsibility for the consequences of that decision on the health and welfare of the Cuban people rests squarely upon the United States.

Long years ago, in a moment of exuberance over the use of American power against a vastly weaker nation, Secretary of State John Hay called the Spanish-American War a "splendid little war." That phrase, and the attitude behind it, have haunted the relations between the United States and Cuba for two generations. And it may be that Hay's splendid little war will turn out to have been the first-stage detonator for a horrible, monstrous conflict.

But if not, the first order of business will still remain the changing of American policy toward Cuba. In this matter, as in others, the responsibility of the historian and the citizen are identical. That responsibility is to act on ex-President Dwight David Eisenhower's reminder on October 23, 1962, that "we are free to ask and to learn how we arrived at our present state, even in foreign policy."

That has been the purpose of this essay, and of this postscript.

October 24, 1962

William Appleman Williams is Professor of American History at the University of Wisconsin. His professional interests are primarily in American diplomacy, and in the interaction between economics and ideas. He was graduated from the United States Naval Academy in 1944 and served in the amphibious corps during the war in the Pacific. He has also been a carpenter, a jazz drummer, and an organizer for the NAACP in the deep south.